BILLS OF RIGHTS

T5-AFH-468

A COMPARATIVE CONSTITUTIONAL ANALYSIS

Second Edition

MICHAEL LUIS PRINCIPE, J.D., Ph.D.

Professor of Political Science, William Paterson University
Visiting Fellow, St. Edmund's College, Cambridge University

KENDALL/HUNT PUBLISHING COMPANY
4050 Westmark Drive   Dubuque, Iowa 52002

Cover image © Condor 36, 2008. Used under license from Shutterstock, Inc.

Copyright © 2000, 2009 by Michael Luis Principe

ISBN 978-0-7575-5389-9

Kendall/Hunt Publishing Company has the exclusive rights to reproduce this work,
to prepare derivative works from this work, to publicly distribute this work,
to publicly perform this work and to publicly display this work.

All rights reserved. No part of this publication may be reproduced,
stored in a retrieval system, or transmitted, in any form or by any
means, electronic, mechanical, photocopying, recording, or otherwise,
without the prior written permission of the copyright owner.

Printed in the United States of America
10 9 8 7 6 5 4 3 2 1

CONTENTS

PREFACE

Over the course of the past three decades, I have had some incredible opportunities. My undergraduate studies at Whitman College and law school experiences at the University of Washington provided me with many valuable insights and perspectives into international law and society. Then, as a graduate student at the University of California, Santa Barbara, I had the great fortune to be a student of and teaching assistant to Professors *C. Herman Pritchett, Stanley Anderson*, and *Gordon E. Baker*. It was during this period that I greatly expanded my research into the fields of comparative constitutional law, rights, and theory. Later, as a Fulbright Scholar to New Zealand for Dissertation Research, I was present for the debates, enactment, and initial judicial interpretations of the New Zealand Bill of Rights Act 1990. Then, beginning in 1993, as Visiting Scholar at St. Edmund's College, Cambridge University, I witnessed the years of debates and struggles over the incorporation of the European Convention of Human Rights into British law, culminating in the enactment of the Human Rights Act 1998.

With the first edition of this book in 2000, I attempted to examine some of the constitutional traditions and civil liberties developments in four states observing a *common law tradition*, Canada, New Zealand, the United Kingdom, and the United States. My goal was to produce a book that would develop in the reader a basic understanding of and interest in comparative law and rights, with the hope it would also inspire them to expand their research into a field of study I find both fascinating and frustrating.

This second edition of the book attempts to broaden the analysis of the first edition by, first, updating and expanding on the constitutional and jurisprudential evolutions of civil liberties protections in the same four states observing a *common law tradition* and, second, adding a new section which examines the constitutional history and rights development of four states observing a *civil law tradition*, France, Germany, Italy, and Spain.

As the world slowly evolves into a global society, these comparisons become more and more important. Issues such as: whether rights are better protected in a system possessing an entrenched constitution; or is it necessary for ordinary judges to possess the power of judicial review; or are social and economic rights as valuable as civil and political rights are questions the comparative rights scholar must examine and debate. I hope that this edition will help the reader better understand these issues and, at the same time, inspire them to commence further research in the discipline.

Since such a project requires the aid of many people, I must thank the following people for their very generous aid in helping me produce this work. First, I want to thank *David Wills*, Squire Law Librarian at Cambridge University, and *Peter Zawada*, Associate Law Librarian at Cambridge University, for their continuing and unending support in my ongoing research into the mysteries of comparative rights. Second, I wish to thank *Professor Paul Luzio*, Master, *Dr. Michael Robson*, Dean, and *Professor Sir Brian Heap*, former Master of St. Edmund's College, for their years of generosity and support in my research. Third, I wish to thank *Professor Emeritus Peter Juviler* of Barnard College, Columbia University and *Professor George Andreopoulos* of the Graduate Center, City University of New York, for their insightful comments on the need to incorporate the European civil law, as well as social and economic, perspective into the second edition.

Finally, I must thank my family (*Nancy, Michael, Steven, Meghann, Camille, and Isabella*) for their continual support of my late nights and weekends at the computer, as well as for my summer research visits to Cambridge (my home away from home). I could never have completed this project without them. This book is dedicated to them!

CHAPTER 1
DEMOCRACY AND RIGHTS

Let me add that a bill of rights is what the people are entitled to against every government on earth, general or particular, and what no just government should refuse, or rest on inference.
Thomas Jefferson[1]

One of the profound developments of the 20th century was the general acceptance of the idea that democracy means more than the will of the majority. Inherent in this new definition is the view that fundamental rights and freedoms must be available to all citizens if a nation is to consider itself truly democratic. Although the specific protections accorded individuals today are as varied as the languages they speak, a number of rights have been accepted as basic by many governments. These include the rights to human dignity, personal freedom, equality, due process, and welfare.

Since World War II there has been an explosion of rights documents around the world. Whether on the international level, such as the Universal Declaration of Human Rights and the International Covenant on Economic, Social and Cultural Rights, or the national level, such as the Canadian Charter of Rights and Freedoms and the Basic Law for the Federal Republic of Germany, nations have begun recognizing fundamental civil liberties. The result is that more than three-quarters of the single-document constitutions in the world have been adopted during this period.

Closely aligned to this notion of fundamental rights and freedoms have been the principles of the rule of law. The **rule of law** refers to the various established legal principles that impose limitations upon the authority of government. As defined by the eminent 19th Century Professor of English Law at Oxford, Albert Venn Dicey, the rule of law:

> [m]eans in the first place, the absolute supremacy or predominance of regular law as opposed to the influence of arbitrary power, and excludes the existence of arbitrariness, of prerogative, or even of wide discretionary authority on the part of the government.... It means, again, equality before the law, or the equal subjection of all classes to the ordinary law of the land administered by the ordinary courts...[2]

It is in observing the principles of the rule of law that a nation begins to look past the racial, gender, or economic differences among its citizens. By treating each individual equally and fairly, rather than valuing wealth or power, a nation demonstrates the respect and importance it places on its citizens.

In the area of rights, the word **liberty** has played a number of roles throughout the centuries. As stated by Montesquieu, "There is no word that admits of more various significations, and has made more different impressions on the human mind, than that of Liberty."[3] Individuals have used it to unite people against tyrannical governments, states have used it to unite citizens to support state policies, and courts have used it to protect both individual rights and corporate rights. Thus, the concept of liberty has been open to a variety of interpretations, some constructive, some destructive.

At the heart of these interpretations has been the notion that an individual should have the freedom to do things as they please, without too many restrictions. Yet, in the past half-century, political and legal theory has shifted towards the belief that in order to provide an *opportunity* for *every* individual to flourish in society, the concept of *liberty* must be combined with the concept of *equality*. In this manner, people from a variety of racial and economic backgrounds can have the chance to find success in society.

Although we are still far away from settling the debate over what is an *equal opportunity*, the progress achieved in the past half-century has been as a result of a number of factors. One factor has been the influence of certain state leaders who have inspired civil rights legislation, in an attempt to give each of their citizens equal rights to the benefits of the nation they swear allegiance to. A second has been the decisions of certain courts that have expanded the definitions of rights by progressively interpreting laws and constitutions. It has been in those jurisdictions where a combination of factors has occurred that rights protections have made the greatest gains.

Among the industrialized western democracies, the first state to constitutionalize civil rights and civil liberties within an entrenched (supreme, higher law) document was the United States, with the ratification of the American Bill of Rights in 1791. Although history has shown that the expansion of those substantive rights took nearly two centuries to develop, the fact that the *principles* underlying those rights were pronounced in a constitutional document during the 18th century and then continuously recognized as constitutionally enforceable is monumental.

Yet, whereas in the United States, constitutional provisions protecting individual liberties were in place long before state and federal legislatures began to systematically address health, safety, and welfare needs, in most liberal democracies, the modern welfare state was already fully developed before their rights documents were adopted. For example, France and Germany enacted legislation regulating factories, commerce, social welfare, and public utilities in the late 19th century, well before their constitutional rights protections were enacted.[4] Thus, the issue of affirmative rights has been central to any modern discussion of fundamental rights and freedoms.

As a result of these historical differences, individuals living in the United States generally talk of their rights "against" governmental intrusions, while citizens living in modern welfare democracies generally talk of the state's "obligations" to provide certain entitlements. Among the various social and economic entitlements Europeans assume government must provide are "the subsidization of child-raising families, and the funding of health, employment, and old age insurance at levels most Americans find scarcely credible."[5] In many respects, this reliance on the welfare state is also the main reason why there has been a general lack of support in some nations for the need of civil liberties protections. It has been assumed that, since government already provides for so many basic needs, it would naturally also put a priority on protecting the rights of citizens. Nevertheless, the great majority of rights documents that have been enacted since World War II have included both civil liberties protections against governmental intrusion and affirmative welfare rights.

A comparison of some of the basic provisions of these rights documents and the U.S. Constitution reveals a number of major differences. First, although the majority of the newly enacted documents do include the various speech, assembly, religion, equal protection, and criminal process protections so familiar to Americans, they inevitably seem to exclude property rights, something the framers of the U.S. Constitution held sacred. Second, these recently adopted rights protections cover a number of affirmative welfare rights (such as health insurance and pensions), that have traditionally been left to the private sector in the United States. Third, although most of the European democracies have established special courts to deal only with constitutional questions, they generally have not adopted the system observed in the United States of allowing ordinary citizens to include constitutional questions in their trials before ordinary courts. Even among the few countries that have adopted judicial review, the willingness and degree to which U.S. courts exercise such powers in support of rights are unmatched.

As a result of these distinctions, it seems evident that, on one hand, the United States has been the leader in the development of rights "against" governmental intrusions, while on the other hand, it is drastically behind the times in providing minimal social and economic benefits to its citizens.

Human Rights are rights which the individual has, or should have, in his society. If societies respected these rights adequately, there would be no need for international law and institutions to help protect them.
Louis Henkin[6]

Perhaps the event in history that opened the door to the concept of *international* human rights was the decision of the Allies after WWII to put Nazis on trial before the Nuremberg tribunal for crimes against peace or humanity and war crimes. Whereas prior to this event, legal positivists argued that individuals had no international legal rights with which they could assert against states, "[p]ersuaded that the lessons of Nuremberg should not be forgotten and that human rights should be guaranteed by explicit provisions of international law, the General Assembly of the United Nations in 1948 voted the precepts of the Universal Declaration of Human Rights."[7] Although, as a resolution of the General Assembly, this document did not impose a binding international obligation upon states, some now consider it to have evolved to the status of customary international law. Regardless, it is through this document that much of the world's perception of rights has been defined and, as such, it is "the fundamental document of international human rights, and has claim to be one of the most important international instruments of the Twentieth Century."[8]

It is in the document's first phrase of the Preamble that its precedent is established: "Whereas recognition of the inherent dignity and of the equal and inalienable rights of all members of the human family is the foundation of freedom, justice, and peace in the world..."[9] Among the Universal Declaration's specific rights that would perhaps be more familiar to Americans are the rights to life, liberty and security of person;[10] to equal protection of the law;[11] to be presumed innocent;[12] to privacy;[13] to marry;[14] to own property;[15] and to freedom of thought, conscience, religion,[16] opinion, expression,[17] peaceful assembly and association.[18] But there are also additional rights in the document that some Americans might find foreign, and yet are very familiar to citizens residing in other western democracies. Among these rights are the right to social security (including those economic, social and cultural rights indispensable to the dignity of the individual);[19] the right to equal pay for equal work;[20] and the right to rest and leisure.[21] Perhaps most importantly, the Declaration includes "the right to a standard of living adequate for the health and well-being of himself and of his family, including food, clothing, housing and medical care and necessary social services, and the right to security in the event of unemployment, sickness, disability, widowhood, old age or other lack of livelihood in circumstances beyond his control."[22]

Once the Declaration was proclaimed, "states began the task of creating a legally-binding covenant that would implement the rights proclaimed in it."[23] Early in the drafting process, economic and social rights were added to the covenant's recognition of political and civil rights. In response, Britain and the United States argued that these new rights were actually aspirations, rather than rights (since their realization was determined by available resources and controversial economic theories) and should not be included within a covenant honoring civil and political rights. As a result, the covenant was divided into two parts, one addressing civil and political rights, and the other addressing economic, social, and cultural rights.

In 1966, the United Nations adopted both the International Covenant on Civil and Political Rights (ICCPR) and the International Covenant on Economic, Social and Cultural Rights (ICESCR). When combined, the two covenants made the rights stated in the *Universal Declaration* binding on any states who sign the treaties. However, since each of the treaties had to be ratified by a sufficient number of states before they entered into force, it took another decade before they achieved that status. Together, the Universal Declaration, ICCPR, and ICESCR have become known as the International Bill of Rights.

The ICCPR, which entered into force on 23 March 1976, contains two Optional Protocols. One protocol establishes a mechanism whereby individuals can submit complaints (communications), while the second protocol abolishes the death penalty. In 1992, the United States finally ratified the ICCPR, but not before the Senate had declared "the provisions of Article 1 through 27 of the Covenant are not self-executing."[24] This declaration made it so individuals were prohibited from bringing a cause of action for violation of these rights unless and until Congress enacts specific legislation implementing the treaty. As a result, although the United States can now claim it has ratified the ICCPR, in reality (as it is not included within its domestic laws) for all intents and purposes the United States is in the same situation it was before ratifying the treaty.

The ICESCR, which entered into force on 3 January 1976, covers far more expansive rights than the ICCPR and requires a greater demand on available resources in order to observe these rights. Despite this, 155 states have ratified this treaty, although one notable exception is the United States. Presidents Nixon and Ford took no action on the treaty after the U.S. representative to the United Nations voted in favor of the Covenant in 1966. President Carter did sign the treaty but the Senate never voted on it and, while Presidents Reagan, George

H.W. Bush, and George W. Bush opposed ratification, President Clinton did little to advance it.

Over the course of the past few decades, a number of other human rights instruments have entered into the international arena. Among them are the Convention on the Elimination of All Forms of Racial Discrimination; the Convention on the Elimination of All Forms of Discrimination Against Women; the United Nations Convention Against Torture; the Convention on the Rights of the Child; the International Convention on the Protection of the Rights of All Migrant Workers and Members of their Families; and the Rome Statute of the International Criminal Court.

Yet none of the international human rights instruments so far mentioned have had the monumental impact a certain regional Convention has. Having just escaped the ravages of WWII, Europe was suddenly feeling the challenges being presented by the seizure of certain Eastern European states by Communist forces. In response, proposals for a European organization possessing the power to protect human rights were being offered and, after a draft Convention was prepared in 1950, The European Convention for the Protection of Human Rights and Fundamental Freedoms (*Convention*) was signed in 4 November 1950 in Rome. Ratified by a tenth state on 3 September 1953, the *Convention* entered into force.

Among the various rights included in the *Convention* are the rights: to life;[25] to not be subjected to torture or to inhuman or degrading treatment or punishment;[26] to liberty and security of person;[27] to a fair and public hearing;[28] to be free from the application of ex post facto laws;[29] to respect for private and family life;[30] to freedom of thought, conscience, religion,[31] expression[32] and peaceful assembly;[33] and to marry.[34] However, the reason this organization has been so successful is because of its international legal procedures for enforcing these rights. Having established the European Court of Human Rights (ECHR) and the European Commission of Human Rights (which were merged under the *Convention's* Protocol 11 in 1994, with the Commission being phased out in 1999), states could petition for breaches of *Convention* provisions beginning in 1953 and (what was a radical departure from the International Court of Justice), *individuals* could petition for relief of *Convention* violations beginning in 1955. Although, initially, states had to recognize the right of individual petition for their nationals, it became so automatic by 1994 that the state option was deleted by Protocol 11.

As a result of the acceptance of ECHR judgments by European states, there have been a notable number of human rights successes achieved by the Court. No other regional organization on the planet has had the impact or influence on human rights that the Convention and Court have had in Europe. This has occurred despite the challenges of balancing a variety of conflicting domestic state courts and laws. Of course, the positive impact did not come overnight. In the Court's first substantive decision the *ECHR* chose to allow Ireland to derogate from the *Convention* (under Article 15) by declaring their actions were taken as extraordinary measures to combat a public emergency. Thus, in the *Lawless* case, detaining an IRA suspect for five months without trial was not a violation of Articles 5 and 6 of the *Convention*.[35] It was not until 1968 that the Court, in *Neumeister*,[36] finally issued a decision against a member state. "The Court held that Austria's detention without trial for 26 months of a businessman accused of tax fraud violated Article 5's guarantees to a trial within a reasonable time or to a release pending trial."[37]

But it was with the *Sunday Times* judgment[38] that the ECHR earned its reputation as a powerful protector of human rights. Attempting to pressure the manufacturer and distributor of the drug thalidomide into settling a decade long case out-of-court, The *Sunday Times of London* sought to publish an article describing the legal proceedings that had occurred up to that point, as well as the fact that during this same time, children who had taken the drug were suffering physical defects as a result. Since these children were not receiving their much needed, but expensive medical care during this litigation, the *Times* was prepared to go to print. When the British Government obtained an injunction from the courts restraining The *Sunday Times* from publishing the article, and the subsequent House of Lords appeal unanimously upheld the injunction, the paper then went to the European Commission claiming the injunction violated their Article 10 (freedom of expression) rights under the *Convention*. In two very controversial decisions, first the European Commission (8-5), and then the ECHR (11-9) ruled in favor of the paper. Since the United Kingdom had accepted the jurisdiction of the Court, as well as the individual right to petition process, it was forced to abide by the decision and pay the judgment.

It is in this process of overseeing the protection of rights across state boundaries that the ECHR contributes greatly to the ongoing development of international law. Like the courts in Canada and the United States that possess the power of judicial review and can invalidate unconstitutional actions by their governments, the ECHR has the power to tell the executive branches of *Convention* member states that their actions are in violation of *Convention* rights. Regardless of whether these member states observe a common law tradition or a civil law tradition, the Court has been granted, and in some cases assumed, these powers. Thus, although the age-old argument (that it is undemocratic to give the judiciary the power to invalidate actions of the executive and legislative branches of government) is accurate on one level, the resulting decisions of the courts may in fact be quite democratic. For example, these decisions may protect the due process rights of an individual so that they are free from arbitrary detention, or they may protect a particular person's equal access to certain social security benefits, or they may protect the free expression rights of a person so that the public has the benefit of knowing all of the pertinent information in a debate, or they may protect an individual's access to the political process so that their opinion can be registered.

As the subsequent chapters of this book attempt to show, despite the fact that each of these various states (France, Germany, Italy, Spain, Canada, New Zealand, the United Kingdom, and the United States) have their own domestic laws and rights machinery, individuals are (or at least should be) the important factors in civil society today and this process of protecting individual rights will continue to evolve.

---

[1] *Letter from Thomas Jefferson to James Madison* (Dec. 20, 1787) quoted in Alpheus Mason & Gordon E. Baker, eds. FREE GOVERNMENT IN THE MAKING: READINGS IN AMERICAN POLITICAL THOUGHT (4th ed. 1985) p.285.

[2] INTRODUCTION TO THE STUDY OF THE LAW OF THE CONSTITUTION (MacMillian, 10th ed. 1961) p.42.

[3] THE SPIRIT OF THE LAWS [as quoted in Mason & Baker, *supra* n.1, p47].

[4] Glendon, Mary Ann, *Interdisciplinary Approach: Rights in Twentieth-Century Constitutions*, 59 U. CHICAGO LAW REVIEW 519, 521 (1992).

[5] Glendon, *supra* n.4, p.525.

[6] Henkin, Louis, Neuman, Gerald, Orentlicher, Diane, & Leebron, David. HUMAN RIGHTS (Foundation Press, 1999) p.302.

[7] Janis, Mark W. AN INTRODUCTION TO INTERNATIONAL LAW, 4th Ed. (Aspen, 2003) p.259.

[8] Henkin…, *supra* n.6, p.286.

[9] Universal Declaration of Human Rights, G.A. Res. 217A, U.N. Doc. A/810, at 71 (1948).

[10] Article 3

[11] Article 7

[12] Article 11

[13] Article 12

[14] Article 16

[15] Article 17

[16] Article 18

[17] Article 19

[18] Article 20

[19] Article 22

[20] Article 23

[21] Article 24

[22] Article 25

[23] Henkin…, *supra* n.6, p.321.

[24] 138 Cong. Rec. S4781-84 (1992).
[25] Article 2
[26] Article 3
[27] Article 5
[28] Article 6
[29] Article 7
[30] Article 8
[31] Article 9
[32] Article 10
[33] Article 11
[34] Article 12
[35] ECHR (1 July 1961, ser.A, no.3).
[36] ECHR (27 June 1968, ser.A, no.8).
[37] Janis, *supra* n.7, p.271.
[38] ECHR (26 April 1979, ser.A, no.30).

CHAPTER 2
THE HISTORY OF THE COMMON LAW SYSTEM
AND THE DEVELOPMENT OF PARLIAMENTARY SUPREMACY
AND JUDICIAL REVIEW

Prior to the Norman Invasion, led by William the Conqueror in 1066, Anglo-Saxon England had a fairly well developed system of handling civil and criminal legal matters. Although lacking a central court, the country was divided up into shires (counties) that had historically been separate kingdoms. "The king administered the shires through the person of the shire reeve (sheriff)....The sheriff was the king's principal judicial and administrative officer at the local level. Sheriffs collected taxes, urged support of the king's administrative and military policies, and performed limited judicial functions."[1] One of the ways the Anglo-Saxon king would implement policy was to issue **writs** (written orders containing the royal seal). Writs were used for a variety of purposes, including awarding land to faithful subjects, instructing courts to convene, or directing a sheriff to take some specific action.[2]

After the Anglo-Saxon king, Edward the Confessor, died in 1066, the Witan (an assembly of powerful nobles) elected Edward's brother-in-law Harold, Earl of Wessex, king. Claiming to be the rightful heir to the crown, William (Duke of Normandy and Edward's cousin) responded by invading England, defeating the Anglo-Saxons, and assuming the throne. Recognizing he had inherited a working legal system throughout the country, William announced that the customary laws and regional courts would continue to be observed during his reign. But, in order to gain the loyalty of his new subjects (particularly the more powerful barons and lords), William claimed all of the property in England was owned by the Crown and "in 1086 he required all landowners to swear allegiance to him."[3] Thus, although the Anglo-Saxons had initiated a form of feudalism, "for William I the problem of maintaining order and earning tax revenue was found in the creation of a feudal system that centralized royal power by devising a legal system for resolving private disputes among the landowners."[4]

Perhaps the most important step in the development of the common law system was the evolution of writs. What began simply as a written order by the king, eventually developed into a series of highly specific petitions requesting legal action. As these petitions expanded in number, they evolved into a catalogue of basic forms.[5] During the 13th century, Henry Bracton, an English lawyer, was one of the first to collect cases. His treatise on the administration of the law through writs, which was based upon cases collected from over two decades, became one of the most influential legal works of the early common law.[6]

Yet, there were a number of other important steps that occurred during the common law's development. For example, the concept of "a law of the land" originated with the signing of the Magna Carta of 1215 between the king and his baronial enemies. This resulted in a permanent body of law that everyone, including the king, had to respect. Also important was the establishment of a centralized court system, including the Court of the King's Bench, the Court of Common Pleas (which dealt with civil disputes generally), and the Exchequer (which dealt with fiscal matters).

As the courts became less flexible in resolving disputes, particularly those issues requiring a remedy besides damages, people began to appeal to the king for justice. The king transferred the appeals to the Chancery (a department which handled the paperwork of the government) for review. There, the chancellor, who was usually a Roman and canon law educated cleric, would investigate and then shape a remedy. Through this process, courts of equity were developed and remedies (such as injunctions, specific performance, and trusts) were established.[7]

Another major system of courts during this period was the ecclesiastical courts. As this system had been developed by the Catholic church in Italy, it was largely influenced by Roman and Italian law. These courts maintained jurisdiction over inheritance and marriages, as well as over all religious matters.

Through the years, as the common law evolved, this process of interpreting and applying writs resulted in judges beginning to rely on prior judgments announced in similar cases. Such reliance provided the system of justice with more consistency and predictability. Thus, the doctrine of **judicial precedent** (*stare decisis*) was born and the position of judge became the dominant figure in the common law system.[8]

Among the more important people to provide early insight into the common law system were Thomas Littleton (15th century), Edward Coke (16th century), and William Blackstone (18th century). In *Dr. Bonham's case* (1610), Chief Justice Lord Coke announced the rule that any statute which is contrary to common right and reason is controlled by the common law and therefore invalid. This meant, if a decision by a judge at common law conflicted with a statute enacted by Parliament, the statute must be ruled null and void. Although this view was accepted for decades (opening up the possibility for a divided law-making sovereignty between legislative and judicial branches), it eventually was rejected in favor of parliamentary supremacy, thus eliminating the argument for absolute English judicial independence.[9]

Sir William Blackstone, a professor at Oxford, published his *Commentaries on the Laws of England* in 1765. In his *Commentaries*, Blackstone argued that, rather than creating new law by incorporating their personal values and priorities into decision-making, judges are duty bound to simply decide issues before them on the basis of the law of the land.[10] In addition, as natural law was a significant component of the law, Blackstone argued that any human law which is contrary to natural law is invalid.[11]

The Doctrine of Parliamentary Supremacy

The system of government that evolved in Great Britain, subsequent to the English Revolution and Act of Settlement, was one observing the doctrine of parliamentary supremacy. The doctrine of parliamentary supremacy originated in the political philosophy of Thomas Hobbes and was developed by William Blackstone and Albert Venn Dicey.[12]

According to Blackstone, the legislative authority of Parliament in this system "can, in short, do everything that is not naturally impossible; and therefore some have not scrupled to call its power, by a figure rather too bold, the omnipotence of parliament."[13] As a result, although Albert Venn Dicey suggested both an external limitation on Parliament's sovereignty (the possibility of a majority of subjects ignoring a law) and an internal limitation (the fact that even a despot's character is molded by the social environment around them),[14] the fundamental premise of this system is that no power on earth can set aside the legislation of Parliament.

Dicey attempted to explain the nature of parliamentary supremacy by showing that its existence is legal fact and that Parliament is an absolutely sovereign legislature. For Dicey, Parliament included the king, House of Lords, and House of Commons, which together were described as the King in Parliament. Under the principle of parliamentary supremacy, Dicey argued that Parliament has "the right to make or unmake any law whatever; and further, that no person or body is recognized by the law of England as having a right to override or set aside the legislation of Parliament."[15]

As for the argument that there are some limitations on the legislative sovereignty of Parliament, Dicey responded that, although the judiciary has had a major impact in the development of the common law, parliamentary supremacy restricts judges from claiming any power to repeal statutes. In addition, Parliament even has the power to regulate or abolish the powers of the Crown or the executive government if it so chooses. Finally, as for limiting the authority of its successors, Dicey maintained that any attempt to bind future Parliaments would severely disable them from considering all available options in legislating for the public welfare. Therefore, because the cornerstone of Britain's constitution is the doctrine of the legislative supremacy of Parliament, none of these limitations can be considered legitimate.

The ideological roots for this concentration of powers in the sovereignty of Parliament, as reasoned by the eminent British legal scholar Geoffrey Marshall, are found in the writings of Thomas Hobbes.[16] Hobbes argued that humans are generally rational, self-interested beings who are driven by their desires. Since power is the mechanism by which humans can satisfy their desires, they are constantly in pursuit of power. Unfortunately, power is scarce, which leads to competition and results in a war of all against all. This would be most evident in a state of nature, where there is no sovereign power.

The final characteristic in Hobbes' view is that humans are all equal. They each have their own, equally valid, understanding of what is good and they all are equally vulnerable to sudden and violent death. Therefore, in order to escape from this horrible state of nature, humans must agree to a social contract, whereby they lay down their right to self-government in order to create one sovereign authority. For Hobbes, humans must agree to transfer all of their alienable rights to the sovereign because, if sovereignty is not absolute, society will fall into civil war and humans will return to a state of nature, where life is solitary, poor, nasty, brutish, and short.[17] This then, was the philosophical justification for concentrating all sovereign powers into one authority, Parliament.

The Doctrine of Judicial Review

Judicial review is the power of a court to review the acts of the executive and legislative branches and declare them unconstitutional. Although this power is not specifically provided for in the United States Constitution, because a number of state courts were already applying judicial review in state court decisions, the framers took it for granted that the United States Supreme Court would also eventually assume such powers.[18]

James Madison and Alexander Hamilton were two of the framers who supported the Supreme Court's assumption of the power of judicial review. While Madison considered this power important in alleviating situations that could lead to rebellion,[19] Hamilton argued that judicial review is essential to preventing legislative oppression. In The Federalist Papers: No.78, he stated "that the courts were designed to be an intermediate body between the people and the legislature, in order, among other things, to keep the latter within the limits assigned to their authority…..Nor does this conclusion by any means suppose a superiority of the judicial to the legislative power. It only supposes that the power of the people is superior to both; and that where the will of the legislature, declared in its statutes, stands in opposition to that of the people, declared in the Constitution, the judges ought to be governed by the latter rather than the former. They ought to regulate their decisions by the fundamental laws, rather than by those which are not fundamental."[20]

Finally, in the 1803 case of *Marbury v. Madison*,[21] Chief Justice John Marshall and the remaining justices of the Supreme Court formally assumed the power of judicial review. Interestingly, the Court came to this decision despite the fact that it was clearly the weakest branch of government, that the Jefferson Administration was vehemently opposed to their assumption of this power, and that there were no assurances the decision would even be respected. Yet, the result of this decision is that it forms the foundation for the most powerful tool in the arsenal of the Court, judicial authority to invalidate acts of coordinate branches of government.

Over the course of the first century and a half after *Marbury*, while the constitutional jurisprudence of the United States expanded dramatically through the application of judicial review, few other nations incorporated the doctrine into their systems of government. Then, at the conclusion of WWII, a number of countries observing a civil law tradition chose to institutionalize judicial review into their constitutions, partly in response to their recent histories with uncontrolled executive power, and partly due to the American influences during occupation. The one major difference in the European style of judicial review was that, rather than providing judicial review powers to ordinary judges (as in the United States), these states established special constitutional courts whose sole function is to examine constitutional questions from public authorities, ordinary courts, and/or individual citizens and issue a decision on that issue only.[22]

The British Constitution and Rights

The constitution of the United Kingdom demonstrates just how much power resides with Parliament. Unlike the entrenched, supreme law constitutions of Canada and the United States, the UK constitution is not a single written document. Rather, it is a combination of various statutes and conventions, as well as the principles of the rule of law. Constitutional documents in the United Kingdom include the Magna Carta of 1215, the Petition of Right of 1628, the Bill of Rights of 1689, the Act of Settlement 1701, and (more recently) the Human Rights Act 1998. Although (similar to other common law states), the major source of English law for centuries emanated from the caselaw decisions of judges, over the course of the last 150 years, legislative enactments have become the primary source of law. Thus, the powers of the legislative branch in a system observing parliamentary supremacy (as compared to a system observing an entrenched constitution, checks and balances, and judicial review) are tremendous.

As Parliament's power shifted from the definition Dicey envisioned (comprising the king, House of Lords, and House of Commons) to one where generally all power resides in the House of Commons, one criticism that has increasingly been leveled against this system is that it is does not protect civil rights well. In the 1990s, these criticisms developed into protests when a variety of groups called for radial change in the British political system. John Smith, the late Labour Party leader, reversed decades of Labour opposition to a bill of rights when he announced support for such a document.[23] The Liberal Democrats Party also requested political change while arguing for incorporation of the European Convention into municipal law.[24] Then there was the Charter 88 Campaign, which organized tens of thousands of signatories to its call for constitutional change and reform.[25]

At the center of these movements was the debate over parliamentary supremacy and its potential to protect fundamental rights and freedoms. As stated by British constitutional scholar, Rodney Brazier, "Many people in the United Kingdom have come to believe that human rights are now much better protected in many foreign legal systems than they are in Britain."[26] According to Ronald Dworkin, Professor of Jurisprudence at University College London and New York University School of Law, this is exactly the case. He maintained that the British government, particularly under Prime Minister Thatcher, continually extinguished civil liberties whenever those rights conflicted with political whim. As evidence of this, Dworkin cites the fact that, between 1965 and 1990, Britain had twice as many petitions lodged against it and it lost more serious cases before the European Court of Human Rights than any other nation. Freedoms of privacy, protest, and speech, as well as criminal procedure protections, have all been sacrificed within Britain's system of legislative sovereignty.[27]

As a result of these efforts to reform constitutional rights protections, the Labour government, under Prime Minister Tony Blair, promised dramatic changes. In subsequently publishing a White Paper entitled *Rights Brought Home*, the Government set out its case for a human rights bill that would incorporate the European Convention on Human Rights into municipal law. The goal of this incorporation was to "strengthen representative and democratic government.......

by enabling citizens to challenge more easily actions of the state if they fail to match the standards set by the European convention."[28] This was in direct response to the heavy emotional and financial burdens suffered by many British citizens who had had their *Convention* rights violated by the government but were then forced to seek relief outside Britain. According to the Home Department, these individuals have had to spend "on average five years and 30,000 pounds to get an action into the European Court at Strasbourg once all domestic remedies have been exhausted."[29]

Supporters of the human rights bill centered their arguments on the liberal traditions of the English Bill of Rights and American Declaration of Independence,[30] the importance of civil liberties protections,[31] the necessity to preserve the sovereignty of Parliament,[32] the benefits British citizens would reap from being able to seek redress in their own courts,[33] and the fact the judiciary would only be empowered to declare legislation incompatible with the *Convention*. They would not be able to strike down laws.[34] In addressing the various bills of rights models the Government studied, Mr. Jack Straw stated, "We examined how Canada and New Zealand.....had dealt with similar issues and whether a Bill of Rights could appropriately be entrenched as a basic and fundamental law with a higher status than the law passed by their Parliaments. We decided to reject Canada's approach, which was, in effect, to establish a fundamental law that, in certain circumstances, took precedence over laws passed by its Parliament. We also considered the New Zealand model. We came up with our own approach – it is a British answer to a British problem – fundamental to which is the sovereignty and supremacy of Parliament."[35]

In response to the proposal, opponents generally argued the document would impose limitations on the sovereignty of Parliament,[36] grant the judiciary unprecedented powers,[37] and be worthless in protecting civil liberties.[38] For example, as stated by Sir Brian Mawhinney during parliamentary debates, "The Bill is not even about giving human rights to our citizens - they have them already. Whether intentional or not, the Bill is about diminishing the sovereignty of Parliament; it is about weakening our democracy and changing fundamentally the balance of the separation of powers between the Executive, the legislature and the judiciary. The result will be a further increase in the power of the Executive, the diminution of Parliament, and the politicisation of the judiciary."[39]

Despite the variety of arguments offered during parliamentary debates over the Human Rights Bill, the central issue clearly concerned the doctrine of legislative sovereignty. Yet, since World War II, a number of developments in British law have already diminished the sovereignty of Parliament. One of the most important developments was Britain's ratification of the European

Convention on Human Rights in 1951 and its subsequent acceptance of the right of British citizens to bring cases against the government in the European Court of Human Rights. This meant subjecting British law to the determination of foreign judges, which, at a minimum, threatens the foundations of parliamentary supremacy. As previously pointed out by Professor Dworkin, there have been a number of decisions by the European Court against the British government. Some have concerned the treatment of suspected terrorists, while others have involved access to a lawyer for those detained in jail, discrimination in immigration, and protections against indiscriminate wiretapping and covert surveillance.

A second development has been the fact that many of the "leading courts in the Commonwealth, including the Privy Council, have decided that provisions of a basic constitutional document can control future parliaments."[40] Although the courts have not suggested that a legislature can bind its successors as to their future legislative content, they have concluded that should a parliament specify a special procedure for enacting or repealing a statute, it is only assuming its inherent power to change the law affecting itself. Since this concerns legislative process and not content, the courts have maintained that no question of sovereignty arises from such decisions.[41]

A third development has been Britain's membership in the European Union. "Parliament altered the standard Sovereignty doctrine when it incorporated the Treaty of Rome through the European Communities Act 1972, making it clear that there are indeed situations in which the courts can declare even later enacted legislation inoperative if it conflicts with directly applicable European law."[42] Originally conceived in 1951 to exercise control over the coal and steel industries of six western European states, the European Community eventually expanded its focus to include almost all other areas of economic activity and more than twice as many nations. In addition to extensive legal, political, and economic relations between member nations, the institutions of the "Community" have acquired extensive quasi-federal and preemptive legislative powers. Since nations are bound to implement the contents of directives, the growth of Community law has increasingly extended into the previously exclusive domain of state law. According to Professor Emeritus Sir David Williams, "it has become more and more recognised that the House of Lords, through the process of '[m]isapplying' British statutes deemed to be at odds with Community law, has come perilously close to striking down statutes."[43]

The Human Rights Act (HRA) received Royal Assent and became law in November of 1998.[44] In order to prepare judges and magistrates for their responsibilities as interpreters of the *Convention*, a task force under the direction of Home Office Minister Lord Williams was assembled and implementation of the Act was scheduled for October 2, 2000. Some of the specific rights incorporated by the Act include: the right to a fair trial; the right to respect for private and family life, home, and correspondence; the right to freedom of thought, conscience, and religion; the right to peaceful enjoyment of property; the right to freedom of expression; the right to freedom of assembly and association; the right to liberty and personal security; and the right to life.

Perhaps the most controversial part of the HRA is its section 4 (Declaration of Incompatibility, or DOI). As section 4(6) specifies, a court's declaration of incompatibility between an act of Parliament and a *Convention* right "does not affect the validity" of the legislation, nor is it "binding on the parties to the proceeding in which it is made." Rather, such a declaration simply puts the government on notice that there is a conflict between the legislation and the European Convention on Human Rights, thus presenting the government with the opportunity to either rectify the problem or ignore it. "Although the UK Government complied voluntarily with the Law Lords' first DOI in *Anderson* in November 2002, and later with the DOI in *Bellinger* in April, 2003, the HRA's first real test of practical strength would not come until the House of Lords made a DOI with respect to an Act the UK Government was strongly determined not to amend."[45]

As argued by Robert Wintemute, professor of Human Rights Law at King's College London, this occurred with the Belmarsh Prison Case.[46] In this case, the Law Lords ruled that sections of the Anti-terrorism, Crime and Security Act 2001 (the Government's post-9/11 anti-terrorism legislation) were incompatible with Articles 5 (right to physical liberty) and 14 (right to be free from nationality discrimination) of the *Convention* since, even if the evidence is insufficient to establish a "reasonable suspicion" that the suspects had committed a criminal offense, if they are non-United Kingdom nationals but cannot be deported, the legislation permits such persons suspected of terrorism involvement to be detained indefinitely, without criminal charge or trial. Although the Belmarsh prisoners were eventually released and the government enacted the Prevention of Terrorism Act 2005 to comply with the declaration of incompatibility, the government's delay in releasing the prisoners caused Professor Wintemute to state: "the Belmarsh Prison Case demonstrates unequivocally the weakness of section 4 of the HRA in practice. The highest court in the UK had no power to order that the prison cells of the detainees be opened, or that they be compensated for their *Convention*-incompatible detention. For the next three months, only the executive held the key. Fortunately for the detainees, their prison cells also had timers attached that would automatically open the doors. They were finally released in March 2005, but only because the 2001 Act was about to expire, and not, I would argue, because of the Law Lords' DOI. Indeed, it was the legislative House of Lords that had protected them in advance by insisting that the 2001 Act contain a 'sunset clause.'"[47]

In response to the inherent weaknesses in the section 4 (Declaration of Incompatibility) provisions, the European Court of Human Rights ruled in *Hobbs v. UK*[48] that individuals in the United Kingdom are not obligated to exhaust all domestic remedies before complaining to the court in Strasbourg for redress of their *Convention* rights. The court stated: "…the [UK] Government have failed to establish that either of the domestic remedies referred to [including s 4] is sufficiently 'effective' so as to be capable of providing the applicant with redress for his complaint, and so as to require exhaustion…"[49]

Despite the problems with the HRA's Declaration of Incompatibility provisions, since its implementation, the Act has benefited a number of British citizens both in and out of court. As cited by the British Institute of Human Rights (BIHR), among the various instances whereby the HRA has helped citizens protect their rights without having to go to court are:

(1) A family, after complaining about the unexplained bruising their disabled child had received in a hospital, had their concerns dismissed and their visitation rights extinguished. Then, after receiving human rights training from the BIHR, they challenged the hospital on the basis of their son's Article 3 (right not to suffer inhuman or degrading treatment) and Article 8 (right to respect for family life) rights. The result was that the hospital reversed its decision and the parents' visitation rights were reinstated;

(2) After receiving human rights training, a social worker used a woman and her family's Article 2 (right to life) and Article 3 (right to be free from inhuman and degrading treatment) rights as the basis for her argument that a local authority should protect the family from a violent ex-partner. The result was that family was awarded new accommodations; and

(3) A local action group persuaded a local authority to reverse its policy of not providing school transport for physically disabled children with special educational needs by arguing that the students' Article 8 (right to respect for family life) rights include their equal need to get out and take part in social activities as much as any other children.[50]

The British Human Rights Act has also been instrumental in protecting the rights of British citizens in the court room. One example was *Ghaidan v. Mendoza*,[51] where the England and Wales Court of Appeal took the opportunity to go beyond the precedent of the Strasbourg Court and "held that a failure to treat a surviving unmarried same-sex partner in the same way as a surviving unmarried different-sex partner, in relation to succession to a rent-controlled tenancy, was sexual orientation discrimination violating Article 14 of the convention combined with Article 8 (respect for home)." Subsequent to *Mendoza*, the European Court of Human Rights followed suit in a similar case.[52]

Among caselaw examples offered by the British Institute of Human Rights was a 2005 case where the parents of a severely disabled daughter requiring constant nursing, challenged the Primary Care Trust's decision to put her in a residential facility rather than provide care in the parents' home. Arguing that this would infringe on their daughter's Article 8 (right to family life) rights by depriving her of the mental stimulation and confidence they could provide her, the court ordered the Trust to reconsider its decision.[53]

One area where the Law Lord's somewhat narrow view towards the primary aim of the ECHR is evident is with the awarding of damages for *Convention* violations. As stated by Lord Bingham, since the *Convention* was intended to promote fundamental rights among its members, the ECHR's finding of a breach is just satisfaction. According to Lord Bingham, generally, only where actual loss or damage has been caused by a breach does the court award compensation. As a result of this perception, courts in the UK have been reluctant to award damages in HRA cases.[54]

In July of 2006, a *Review of the Implementation of the Human Rights Act* was published by the Department of Constitutional Affairs (DCA). Despite the fact the *Review* determined the HRA had no significant impact on criminal law, it did state that the HRA's effect on the development of governmental policy was significant. It also stated that, because of the HRA, the executive was under greater scrutiny by the courts than before.[55]

Although accepting the supremacy of European Community law through the incorporation of the Treaty of Rome was perhaps the most important constitutional change for Britain of the twentieth century, the Human Rights Act is the most important civil rights reform of the past half century. Not only does it signal British citizens that they can enforce their rights under the European Convention at home, but it also affords the British judiciary the opportunity to begin assuming responsibility for protecting civil liberties in much the same manner as the New Zealand, Canadian, and American courts have done. As stated by Professor Emeritus Sir David Williams of Cambridge University "…the cumulative impact of the changes…may well lead to an assumption of judicial review akin to that in *Marbury v. Madison*…"[56]

The New Zealand Constitution and Rights

Great Britain gained sovereignty over New Zealand through its interpretation of the Treaty of Waitangi, the 1840 agreement between the Maori chiefs and Captain William Hobson, the representative of the Crown. Although scholars have shown that the Maori chiefs were merely ceding governorship, and not sovereignty, to the British,[57] the Maori were eventually dispossessed of their lands and forced to assimilate into British culture as second class citizens by a number of democratically elected governments. By 1987, the Maori owned less than five percent of the nation's lands and made up nearly fifty percent of the prison population, even though they comprised ten percent of New Zealand's population.[58] Thus, although important as a constitutional document,[59] the Treaty of Waitangi has done little to help the plight of the Maori historically.

Until the 20th Century, the major source of law in New Zealand was the judiciary and its pronouncement of the common law. As legislation increased, however, the New Zealand system of government shifted from an adversarial system to one observing the doctrine of parliamentary supremacy, which originated in Great Britain. This system assumes that the power of the legislative branch to make law is absolutely sovereign. Since 1950, when the National government abolished the second Chamber of Parliament, New Zealand's House of Representatives has essentially controlled the government as the only remaining chamber of the legislature.

Some have argued that there are a number of social forces applying pressure to the legislative branch as it exercises its lawmaking function. Included among these social forces are elections, the opposition party, the role of the courts, ministerial and cabinet responsibility to the House of Representatives, and constitutional conventions. Yet, regardless what pressures are put to bear on the legislature, it must be remembered that in a system strictly observing parliamentary supremacy, members of Parliament can develop or extinguish laws as they see fit and there is little anyone can do about it other than elect new representatives.

Like the UK constitution, the New Zealand constitution reflects how much power resides with the House of Representatives. Rather than a single written document, it is a combination of various statutes, conventions, and the principles of the rule of law. By 1990, constitutional documents in New Zealand included the Magna Carta of 1215, the Petition of Right of 1628, the Bill of Rights of 1689, and the Constitution Act of 1986,[60] which provided the central framework for governmental action. Of increasing constitutional importance has been the Treaty of Waitangi.

Conventions are another important constitutional source for states observing parliamentary supremacy. **Conventions** are rules that have evolved and become established through frequent usage and custom over the years. Some become so familiar that they are eventually enacted as statutes. As explained by New Zealand scholar R.D. Mulholland, "Conventions are adhered to and observed for political expediency and respect for tradition and not because some specified sanction will follow on breach."[61] Examples of New Zealand conventions include "the Cabinet system.... the opposition system....[and] the practice of ministerial responsibility."[62]

Finally, the entire constitutional system is governed by the principles of the rule of law. As explained by Albert Venn Dicey, the principles of the rule of law exclude arbitrary and discretionary decision-making, require equality before the law, and allow the constitution to be the result of the ordinary law of the land.[63]

Since laws and conventions change through time, the constitution of a country observing parliamentary supremacy is a never-ending mix of these sources. New Zealand's Constitution is no exception. The New Zealand House of Representatives has enjoyed the ultimate power of deciding what is and is not constitutional for decades. Thus, it was into this constitutional history that the bill of rights was proposed, debated, and enacted.

The initial proposal for a bill of rights in New Zealand was made by the National government in August of 1963, when it introduced a bill based upon the Canadian Bill of Rights of 1960. However, after months of debate in Parliament, the proposed bill of rights was allowed to lapse.

The next effort at incorporating rights protections into constitutional form began with the inclusion of a bill of rights in the Labour party's 1981 Election Manifesto. This proposal gained further prominence in 1984 when the Labour Government's Open Government Policy included a bill of rights component. But it was in 1985, when the Labour Government introduced a White Paper supporting a bill of rights into the New Zealand Parliament, that the debate was elevated to the national level.

Although it was the Labour Government's Minister of Justice, Sir Geoffrey Palmer, who presented the White Paper to Parliament, a number of prominent people were supportive of the proposal. Included among these was Sir Kenneth Keith, a professor of Law at Victoria University and President of the New Zealand Human Rights Commission. As chief architect of the White Paper, Sir Kenneth was convinced that an entrenched bill of rights would elevate fundamental rights and freedoms to their proper place in government. In addressing the bill of rights, he attempted to alleviate fears that the judiciary would become oppressive by showing that judges are primarily concerned with ensuring public bodies observe proper processes within the law. In fact, Sir Kenneth argued that a bill of rights can enhance democratic processes.[64]

This was a dramatic change from his earlier views on the subject. In 1964 Sir Kenneth had adamantly opposed the National Government's proposed Bill of Rights Act on the basis that it would transfer traditional legislative and executive tasks to an unfamiliar judiciary.[65] Yet, after attending the graduate law program at Harvard University, where he witnessed the explosion of civil liberties protections being developed by the U.S. Supreme Court first hand, he returned to New Zealand with a new found respect for entrenched constitutional documents. Like Sir Geoffrey, Sir Kenneth's American educational experiences had a profound effect on his constitutional views.

Over the course of the next few years, debates on the strengths and weaknesses of the proposed bill of rights flourished.[66] Perhaps the two major issues addressed in the debate over the White Paper proposal were: whether a bill of rights bestows too much power on an unelected judiciary and whether legislative oppression can be prevented without a bill of rights.

One of the major opponents to the proposal was the New Zealand Law Society. The Law Society argued that judges are the wrong people to be making such decisions and that determining important issues of policy by way of "the lottery of adversary litigation" is odd.[67] Additional criticisms were offered by Members of Parliament Paul East and D.F. Dugdale. Mr. East suggested that the proposed bill of rights would politicize the judiciary and make the system undemocratic by giving unelected judges the power to set aside legislation enacted by duly elected legislators.[68] Mr. Dugdale argued that the proposal shifts power to a judicial elite, imposes the current views of Parliament on its successors, and assumes the ordinary voter "cannot be trusted to know what is good for him."[69]

On the other side of the debate were Sir Geoffrey Palmer, Dr. Jerome Elkind, and the Rt. Hon. Sir Robin Cooke, President of the Court of Appeal of New Zealand. Sir Geoffrey stated that, although the bill of rights would give the judiciary wider power, the specific guarantees are narrow and consented to by the community and the judges must justify their decisions in writing. Dr. Elkind, a member of the law faculty at the University of Auckland, argued in favor of the restraints a bill of rights would impose on the powers of an elected majority in order to protect minority rights from being trampled. Sir Robin stated that to proclaim such guarantees without putting them in writing is really just paying lip service to them. As for the argument that this proposal is undemocratic, he maintained that the judiciary would be safeguarding democracy by interpreting this bill of rights to protect fundamental rights and freedoms.

After years of investigation, the "Final Report of the Justice and Law Reform Committee on the White Paper" concluded that the public needed further schooling on the subject before such a monumental change in the nation's constitutional system could occur. The committee felt that an entrenched constitutional document, as was proposed in the White Paper, was too drastic a change for a system observing parliamentary supremacy.[70] The committee did recommend, however, that Parliament introduce a bill of rights to the public as an ordinary statute. This, then, was the proposal that Parliament subsequently debated: whether to enact a bill of rights statute along the lines of the Canadian Bill of Rights Act of 1960 or to continue to rely on the government to protect fundamental rights and freedoms.

The parliamentary debates occurred on four separate occasions. Each of the debates included well thought out arguments both for and against the bill of rights. Supporters of the legislation emphasized New Zealand's lack of formal constitutional checks on legislative power as well as its recent tendency to let rights gradually erode. Opponents of the proposed bill of rights focused on the transfer of traditional power from the legislative branch to the judiciary, the uncertainty of entering a new legal era, and the fact that, compared to an entrenched document, this proposal is toothless. It can be downgraded or even extinguished on the whim of the majority party in power.

Although Canada was clearly the main point of reference, having shared a heritage of observing parliamentary supremacy with New Zealand, the parliamentary debates also included various references to the American experience. Judge Learned Hand,[71] President Franklin D. Roosevelt,[72] and U.S. Supreme Court Justice William Brennan[73] were all discussed in Parliament. Sir Geoffrey Palmer, by then prime minister, quoted one of Justice Brennan's justifications for a bill of rights as coming from the need of minorities (which can include any of us at certain times) to be protected from tyrannical majorities.

The Bill of Rights Bill was enacted by a 36-28 margin in the House of Representatives and subsequently assented to by the Governor-General on 28 August 1990. The Act was divided into three parts: general provisions, civil and political rights, and miscellaneous provisions. Included in the document are protections from unreasonable search, seizure, and detention; freedom of religion, association, and expression; minority rights; the right to life; and the right not to be subjected to torture. Although the Act specifically prohibits the judiciary from striking down laws of Parliament, those sections that allow the government to implement good faith affirmative action measures, observe the principles of natural justice, and interpret legislation consistently with the Bill of Rights, provide the judiciary with opportunities to review legislative interpretation.

The New Zealand judiciary quickly assumed an active role in protecting fundamental rights and freedoms through their interpretations of the Bill of Rights. In sharp contrast with the Canadian Supreme Court's interpretations of the Canadian Bill of Rights Act of 1960, the New Zealand courts' initial decisions clearly indicated the judiciary would not limit rights to those already in existence. Instead, the courts chose to be more activist in their deliberations, carving out new areas of rights protections.

The great majority of initial court decisions involving the Bill of Rights Act dealt with criminal procedure. According to New Zealand legal scholar Michael Taggart, this was due to a number of factors. First, "much of criminal law enforcement takes place under common law powers or broad statutory powers." Second, the judiciary considers criminal law and procedure as its own special domain. Third, the senior members of the New Zealand judiciary were particularly enthusiastic about the Bill of Rights Act. Fourth, the common knowledge of the failure of the Canadian Bill of Rights Act 1960 was a valuable lesson.[74]

Three of the initial Court of Appeal decisions addressing criminal procedure were *R. v. Rangi*,[75] *R. v. Kirifi*,[76] and *R. v. Crime Appeals*.[77] In *R. v. Rangi*, section 6 (requiring the preferred interpretation of a statute be consistent with the Bill of Rights) and Section 25 (requiring the defendant be presumed innocent until proven guilty) were relied upon by the Court to quash a conviction and sentence because the jury instructions were improper. As a result, in interpreting the Crimes Act of 1961, the Court ruled that the burden of proof remains with the Crown and not with the defendant to show whether defendant's possession of a knife in a public place was without lawful authority or reasonable excuse.

In *R. v. Kirifi*, section 23 (which addresses the rights of persons arrested or detained) was relied upon by the Court to uphold a lower court's exclusion of evidence because of custodial violations. Although the defendant had been in custody over three hours, the police had failed to advise him of his right to consult and instruct a lawyer without delay. Thus, the lower court's exclusion of videotape of the defendant's oral admissions during an interview was justifiable. The Court of Appeal stated, "It seems to us that, once a breach of section 23 (1) (b) has been established, the trial judge acts rightly in ruling out a consequent admission unless there are circumstances in the particular case satisfying him or her that it is fair and right to allow the admission into evidence."

In *R. v. Crime Appeals*, section 23 was again relied upon to order a rehearing. In this case, a defendant admitted committing aggravated robbery even though he had not been told he was arrested or advised of his rights. Subsequently, another defendant was coerced into making admissions despite his previous requests to consult a lawyer. President Cooke stated, "[T]he Acts must not be construed narrowly or technically, but applied in a realistic way. It is an affirmation of the basic rights of the people in New Zealand, and these rights cannot be hard and fast in their operation. The Act must normally be given primacy, subject only to the clear provisions of other legislation."

Two of the most important cases to be decided by the Court of Appeal in the early years after enactment of the Bill of Rights Act were *Ministry of Transport v. Noort* [78] and *Simpson v. Attorney-General [Baigent's Case].*[79] In *Noort*, the Court reversed a lower court decision ruling that the Transportation Act could not be given an interpretation consistent with section 23 (1) (b) of the Bill of Rights. The Court of Appeal stated that section 6 applied because these Acts were only ambiguous, not inconsistent, and could therefore "reasonably stand together." It also interpreted the section 23 right to legal advice as being a fundamental right by stating, "Internationally there is now general recognition that some human rights are fundamental and anterior to any municipal law, although municipal law may fall short of giving effect to them....the right to legal advice on arrest or detention under an enactment may not be quite in that class, but in any event it has become a widely-recognised right...and one of those affirmed in New Zealand."

In *Baigent*, a new public law cause of action for breach of the Bill of Rights Act was recognized by a majority of the Court of Appeal. This was a major development, especially considering the fact that, during the parliamentary debates, Sir Geoffrey Palmer had explained that "the Bill creates no new legal remedies for courts to grant."[80] Rather than basing it on a private law tort claim, the Court stated that it was a public law action for compensation against the state and therefore not affected by the Crown Proceedings Act of 1950. As a result, although the Crown has express statutory immunity from vicarious liability in tort actions, this case subjects the state to potential liability for abuses of the Bill of Rights Act.

Hopkinson v. Police[81] and *Robert John Condon v. The Queen*[82] are two of the more recent cases involving the Bill of Rights Act 1990. In *Hopkinson*, a Wellington school teacher (who protested a 2003 official visit by the Australian Prime Minister by burning a flag on Parliament grounds) had his conviction, for destroying a New Zealand flag with intent to dishonour it, overturned. The court ruled that (in addition to Hopkinson possessing a s.25 right to be presumed innocent), s.6 requires the Flags, Emblems and Names Protections Act 1981 be read consistently with s.14 (Freedom of Expression) of the Bill of Rights Act 1990. The court found that when the various shades of the meaning of dishonor are considered, and the least restrictive meaning is applied, it does not meet the standard for conviction.

In *Robert John Condon v. The Queen,* Condon was convicted of threatening to kill and attempting to pervert the course of justice after a jury trial in the District Court of Timaru. During the week of trial, after Condon's legal counsel was given permission to withdraw, the judge refused adjournment, and Condon represented himself. Condon appealed claiming that, as the judge's decision breached his right to legal representation as required by s.24 of the Bill of Rights Act 1990, his trial was unfair. The Supreme Court stated that (in all but exceptional circumstances) an accused who represents him/herself on a serious charge (without having declined or failed to exercise their right of legal representation) will not have a fair trial. In this instance, the accused did not dismiss his counsel and yet was denied a reasonable opportunity to arrange alternate representation, which breached s.24. As the Crown could not establish (notwithstanding the absence of representation) that the trial was actually fair, the court ruled it was not persuaded that the trial would actually have been the same with legal representation and therefore quashed the convictions.

In the years since the Bill of Rights Act 1990 was implemented, a number of changes in the legal and political landscape of New Zealand have occurred. Three of the most important changes were: (1) enactment of the Human Rights Act 1993 (which deals with discrimination in New Zealand and governs the work of the N.Z. Human Rights Commission); (2) adoption of a mixed member proportional (MMP) system in the House of Representatives (which is essentially proportional representation combined with single member seats); and (3) enactment of the Supreme Court Act 2003 (which extinguishes the option for appeals to the Judicial Committee of the Privy Council and establishes the N.Z. Supreme Court as the nation's final court of appeal).

Like Canada, the New Zealand judiciary has made dramatic progress in protecting fundamental rights and freedoms in a very short period of time. This is especially remarkable considering the fact that, unlike the Canadian and American rights documents, the New Zealand Bill of Rights is merely an ordinary statute, capable of being modified or extinguished by Parliament at any time. Thus, New Zealand is an example of an activist judiciary assuming the responsibility to protect human rights without the benefit of an entrenched constitutional document.

The Dominion of Canada, as a federation of most of the existing colonies, was established by the British North America Act of 1867. Upon enactment, the United Kingdom assumed control over virtually all substantive matters relating to the Canadian Constitution. In fact, when considered against the Colonial Laws Validity Act of 1865 (which made void any provision of colonial legislation that conflicted with a law by the U.K. Parliament extending to that colony), Canada was prohibited from amending the basic structure of its own constitution.

Through the years it became apparent that, although the United Kingdom Parliament would amend the British North America Act of 1867 at various times, it would generally do so only if requested by the Canadian Parliament. At the same time, the Canadian Parliament requested a change only after seeking and receiving the consent of the provincial legislatures, unless the proposal was purely of a federal nature. This process eventually became a constitutional convention, which is a rule that is developed over time as a result of frequent usage and custom.

Historically, the basis of Canada's political system was parliamentary supremacy, as adopted from the United Kingdom.[83] Parliamentary supremacy requires that the legislature be absolutely sovereign. There are no formal checks on the powers of the legislature, other than elections. This, then, was the system of government Canada chose to adopt.

In 1931, Great Britain recognized the independence of such dominions as Canada and New Zealand in the Statute of Westminster. This law provided that, in order for any further enactments by the British Parliament to apply to the dominions, they must first be expressly requested and assented to by that dominion. Unfortunately, because the provinces in Canada failed to reach an agreement with Parliament regarding the formula for amending the constitution, a specific provision was inserted into the statute allowing the British Parliament power to alter, amend, or repeal the British North America Act, 1867-1930, without Canadian consent. Therefore, unlike the other dominions affected by the Statute of Westminster, the Canadian constitution could still be amended by the British government.

This failure of the provinces and the federal government to reach agreement regarding the amendment process for the constitution frustrated the efforts to shift legislative authority from Great Britain to Canada for over half a century. It was not until 1955, when a legal academic named Pierre Trudeau recommended that the Canadian Constitution "should include a statement of fundamental rights,"[84] that an entrenched document began to become a possibility.

Canada's first major attempt to enact civil liberties protections into federal law was the Canadian Bill of Rights Act of 1960. This law was an ordinary statute that afforded the judiciary the opportunity to take a more activist role in the protection of civil rights. Unfortunately, as evidenced by Justice Ritchie's famous quote in *Robertson... v. The Queen*,[85] the Supreme Court of Canada generally chose to adhere to the doctrine of parliamentary supremacy, thus limiting the development of civil rights protections. Considering any expansion of rights the exclusive domain of the legislature, the Court avoided controversy by adopting a "frozen rights" theory of interpretation, choosing to act simply as an umpire of disputes.[86]

Pierre Trudeau continued his proposal for an entrenched bill of rights as part of Canadian constitutional reform in 1965, after being elected to Parliament, and two years later, as Minister of Justice in the Liberal Government of Prime Minister Pearson. Finally, in 1968, when he became prime minister, Trudeau was able to focus the Government on this idea.

One of the major problems facing Canada during this period was the separatist movement in Quebec. Over the course of the next decade, the movement grew. By the time the Parti Quebecois, led by Rene Levesque, was elected in Quebec, it signaled the beginning of an intense effort towards secession from the Canadian Federation. In response to this threat against national unity, the government proposed an entrenched constitution with a Charter of Rights and Freedoms. The purpose of the proposal was to unite Canada on a common set of values, negating the influence of the separatists. When the Quebec referendum on sovereignty-association was held on 20 May 1980, Prime Minister Trudeau and a number of the provincial premiers lobbied for a "no" vote by promising constitutional reform. The Quebecers voted 60-40 against sovereignty-association.

Although the vote inspired Parliament to proceed with the constitutional reform, a number of problems still needed to be addressed. Perhaps the major problem was the stalemate between the federal government and the provincial premiers on the amending formula. Without reaching an accord during the first series of conferences, Prime Minister Trudeau declared the federal government would unilaterally request passage of the Constitution Act by the United Kingdom Parliament. Since this offended the constitutional convention requiring at least substantial provincial support, the matter was referred to three Courts of Appeal. After their decisions were appealed to the Supreme Court, the Court held that a substantial degree of provincial support was required as a matter of constitutional convention.

As a result of the decision, another conference was held and a negotiated compromise was reached, resulting in the transmittal of the proposed Constitution Act 1982 to the United Kingdom. There, it was enacted by the Houses of Commons and Lords and given Royal Assent on March 29, 1982. Passage of the Canada Act in 1982 extinguished the involvement of the United Kingdom in the constitutional development of Canada.

The Canadian Constitution became the supreme law of the land and authorized the judiciary to strike down any laws violating this document. In addition, the Charter of Rights and Freedoms guaranteed a number of very important legal, political, linguistic, and equality rights to individuals. Among these are the freedoms of assembly, association, expression, and press; protections against unreasonable search and seizure, and arbitrary detainment; provisions for right to counsel and bail; a prohibition against cruel and unusual punishment; requirements of equal protection; provisions for affirmative action programs; the equality of French and English as the official languages; and the recognition of aboriginal and treaty rights.

Once the Canadian Constitution became law, the Supreme Court began protecting rights with a zeal unfamiliar in history to most nations' judiciaries.[87] Against a variety of oppressive legislative intrusions, the Court became the guardian of individual rights and freedoms and subsequently wielded its judicial review powers with incredible vigor. Legislation dealing with drug trafficking,[88] murder,[89] criminal investigations and prosecutions,[90] citizenship and geographical qualifications,[91] competition policy,[92] immigration,[93] and Sunday shopping [94] are just a few of the areas in which the Court invalidated laws on the basis of the principles of the constitution.

It was in the landmark case of *R v. Oakes*[95] that the Supreme Court first established its test for challenging a rule or regulation against the guarantees of the Charter of Rights and Freedoms. Section 1 of the Charter reads: "The Canadian Charter of Rights and Freedoms guarantees the rights and freedoms set out in it subject only to such reasonable limits prescribed by law as can be demonstrably justified in a free and democratic society." *Oakes* established the primary test for determining whether the purpose of the limitation can be *demonstrably justified*. David Edwin Oakes was charged with intended trafficking for being in possession of vials of hash oil and $619.45. Oakes responded by claiming the vials were intended for pain relief and the money was from a $666 workers compensation check. On the basis of the Narcotics Control Act (which shifted the burden onto the accused to prove they were not in possession for

31

trafficking purposes) Oakes was convicted. On appeal, Oakes argued this shift in burden violated his section 11(d) rights of the Charter (presumption of innocence) and could not be *demonstrably justified* under section 1 (limitations clause) of the Charter.

In revising the test, the Supreme Court in *Oakes* placed the initial burden upon a challenger to show that their interest is within one of the guaranteed rights or freedoms of the Charter and that the disputed law infringes on that right as a matter of fact. Once they meet that test, the burden then shifts to the government to justify the law or regulation on the basis of a pressing social objective and the fact that any *limitation* on those rights and freedoms is minimal, proportional, and/or necessary. As a result of the court establishing this section 1 test, there has been significant development in human rights protections in Canada, particularly in the area of criminal prosecution rights.

R v. Keegstra[96] was a landmark freedom of expression case whereby the Supreme Court upheld a criminal code of Canada provision (prohibiting unlawful promotion of hatred against an identifiable group) as constitutional under section 2(b) of the Charter (freedom of expression). James Keegstra was a high school teacher in Alberta charged with violating pertinent sections of the criminal code for promoting hatred against an identifiable group by communicating anti-Semitic statements to his students. Although the court found the pertinent sections of the criminal code in violation of section 2(b) of the Charter (freedom of expression), they were *demonstrably justified* under section 1 (limitations clause) since: the law had a rational connection to its objective, the limitations were not overly broad, and because the seriousness of the section 2(b) violation was not as severe as the content of the hateful expression, which had little of value to protect.

In *Law v. Canada* (Minister of Employment and Immigration),[97] the Supreme Court created the test for establishing equality claims under section 15 of the *Charter* (equality rights). Nancy Law was a 30-year-old widow without dependents who applied for survivor benefits under the Canada Pension Plan and was denied because the benefits are generally reserved for survivors who are 65 years old and over, disabled, or with dependents. She appealed the decision on the basis the age requirement was in violation of section 15(1) of the Charter, which lists age as grounds upon which a person has rights against discrimination. Rather than focus on whether the limitation could be *demonstrably justified* under a section 1 analysis, the Supreme Court developed a new test[98] for section 15, requiring a court to focus its entire analysis on the specific purposes of the section (which are to prevent the violation of essential human dignity and freedom through the imposition of disadvantage, stereotyping, or political or social prejudice, and to promote a society in which all persons enjoy equal recognition at law as human beings or as members of Canadian society, equally capable and equally deserving of concern, respect and consideration) and then unanimously ruled the pertinent sections of the Canada Pension Plan do not violate section 15.

Perhaps the one area of the Canadian Constitution that maintains its historical legacy to parliamentary supremacy is section 33 of the Charter (notwithstanding clause). This section allows the federal and provincial governments to temporarily override *Charter* sections 2 and 7-15 rights for up to five years, subject to renewal. Although the federal government has never invoked this section, the provincial governments of Quebec, Saskatchewan, and Alberta have all invoked the clause. In *Ford v. Quebec (A.G.)*,[99] the Supreme Court struck down part of Quebec's Charter of the French Language (restricting the use of commercial signs in English) on the grounds the pertinent section of the Quebec law violated section 2(b) of the Charter (freedom of expression) and could not be *demonstrably justified* under section 1 of the Charter (limitations clause). In response, the Quebec provincial government passed Bill 178 in 1989 (which did not meet the standards established by the court in *Ford*) and invoked section 33 of the Charter (notwithstanding clause) to shield the law from judicial review for five years.

Canada has achieved a fairly remarkable history of rights protections in a very short period of time. Part of this development is clearly the result of the Canadian Supreme Court taking advantage of the wealth of available U.S. case law covering similar issues.[100] But an even greater reason for this explosion of rights protections is because of the philosophy of those justices on the Supreme Court who initially interpreted the Canadian Constitution. If the composition of the Court had been different, the progress of rights protections might have been substantially slower. As it was, the Court was able to break away from the country's constitutional history in a dramatic and monumental manner.

Regardless of what the judicial philosophies are of the future justices on the Court, the short history of the interpretation of the Canadian Constitution has given merit to the statement by Canadian legal scholar David Beatty that, "[t]he fact is, and whether it is legitimate or not, the constitution in Canada resides less in the words of the text than in the legal and political theory of the judge."[101]

The American Constitution and Rights

Whereas the British and New Zealand systems of government possess unentrenched constitutions and are based on the doctrine of parliamentary supremacy, while the Canadian system possesses an entrenched constitution and is somewhat of a hybrid between parliamentary supremacy and separation of powers, the American system of government combines the concepts of republicanism, separation of powers, checks and balances, and federalism with an entrenched (supreme, higher law) constitution. Fearful of tyrannical majorities (as exhibited by their relationship with England) and state sovereignty (as evidenced by their attempt at shared government under the Articles of Confederation), the framers of the constitution attempted to incorporate many of the ideas emanating from the Enlightenment thinkers, such as John Locke, by designing a government that prevented majority tyranny through the mechanism of representation, and prevented tyranny from other sources by incorporating the principles of separation of powers and checks and balances into the constitution.

Believing that the federal government's delegated powers were very limited, the framers declined to include a bill of rights in the original document. Among the many believing a bill of rights was unnecessary, Alexander Hamilton went so far as to say that a bill of rights "would be an even greater threat to liberty," [102] since to provide specific civil liberties would only limit them. Yet, as the ratification process was developing, it became obvious that many people were dissatisfied with the lack of protections individuals were afforded against the federal government. As a result, some states ratified the constitution only after receiving assurances that civil liberty protections would be incorporated into the document as soon as possible.

It was at this point that Thomas Jefferson undertook the effort to convince James Madison of the necessity for a bill of rights. Although not expressly opposed to a bill of rights, having witnessed the disregard of such documents in the past and believing that the enumeration of such rights could only serve to limit them, Madison did not consider the omission of one a material defect. Nevertheless, after exchanging a series of letters, whereby Jefferson addressed both the strengths and weaknesses of a bill of rights, as well as his notion that the judiciary should be the guardian of these rights, Madison became convinced that civil liberty protections were a necessity. [103]

In order to respond to various critics of the proposed adoption of a bill of rights, Madison assumed the role of proposing the amendments to the House of Representatives. Twelve amendments were eventually approved by the Senate and House and then sent to the states for ratification. Ten of these proposed amendments were ultimately ratified on December 15, 1791. Thus, the first ten amendments to the United States Constitution form the basis for the Bill of Rights.

Freedoms of speech, press, assembly, and religion; the right to be secure from unreasonable searches and seizures; a prohibition against double jeopardy;

the incorporation of due process of law restrictions; a provision for assistance of counsel in criminal trials; and a prohibition against cruel and unusual punishment are a few of the more important civil liberties protected in these amendments. Although it took some time for the concept to develop that the ratification of the Bill of Rights was a great achievement, these provisions have had a tremendous impact on constitutional theory, practice, and history.

Having incorporated into the constitution the civil liberty protections required by so many, all that remained was for the judiciary to assume the role as guardian of the Bill of Rights. This began with the development of judicial review. Although neither provided for nor prohibited in the constitution, the Supreme Court's assumption of judicial review powers in *Marbury v. Madison* marked the foundation for judicial independence and opened the door to true checks and balances among the branches.

The second major issue to be addressed in relation to the Bill of Rights was whether the first eight amendments were applicable to the federal government alone or whether they also applied to the states. Since only two of the amendments specified restrictions upon the United States (the First Amendment and one clause in the Seventh Amendment), the question over this fundamental point was left in doubt. In the 1833 case of *Barron v. Baltimore*,[104] a unanimous Supreme Court resolved the debate by ruling that these amendments were inapplicable to the states. The result of this decision was that individuals could rely on the U.S. Constitution for protections against civil liberties violations by the federal government, but in order to protect themselves against civil liberties infractions by state governments, they would have to rely on their state constitutions.

In the subsequent half-century after *Marbury*, the major role of the Supreme Court was to settle disputes. Thus, although a number of important constitutional cases expanding the powers of the national government were decided, it was not until the ratification of the Civil War Amendments that civil liberties began to enter the constitutional debate on a larger scale.

The Thirteenth, Fourteenth, and Fifteenth Amendments to the constitution were intended to provide the newly freed blacks with the same civil liberty protections as white citizens. While the Thirteenth Amendment abolished slavery and the Fifteenth Amendment gave blacks the right to vote, it was the Fourteenth Amendment that severely limited state powers by imposing on them the privileges and immunities, due process, and equal protection clauses. One of the Fourteenth Amendment's main purposes was to constitutionalize the provisions of the Civil Rights Act of 1866. This Act protected the right to make and enforce contracts; to sue and give testimony in court; to inherit, purchase, sell or lease property; and to enjoy the full and equal benefit of all laws and proceedings for the security of person and property as is enjoyed by white citizens.

The two most important sections of the Fourteenth Amendment are Sections One and Five. Section One provides that:

> …No State shall make or enforce any law which shall abridge the privileges or immunities of citizens of the United States; nor shall any State deprive any person of life, liberty, or property, without due process of law; nor deny to any person within its jurisdiction the equal protection of the laws.

It is this section that formed the basis for limitations on state power and provided the Supreme Court with the opportunity to eventually expand civil liberties protections. As for Section Five, it provides that:

> The Congress shall have power to enforce, by appropriate legislation, the provisions of this article.

This section evidences Congress' broad authority to correct abuses of the Amendment. Later, in enacting the Civil Rights Act of 1875, Congress was even more obvious in its assumption that it can not only redress affirmative state discrimination, but discrimination by private individuals as well.

Yet, when the Supreme Court reviewed the Civil Rights Act of 1875,[105] rather than deferring to the will of the people who ratified the Fourteenth Amendment or to the intentions of the Congress that drafted it, the Court instead substituted its own priorities in interpreting the Amendment. This resulted in Congress being told that they had in fact misunderstood the meanings of the Amendment and the congressional powers pursuant to it. By giving a literal interpretation to the words "no State" shall deny equal protection, the Court ruled that only affirmative state action is prohibited, thereby eliminating the authority of Congress to punish discriminatory actions by private individuals under the Fourteenth Amendment. As observed by the eminent 20th century constitutional scholar, C. Herman Pritchett, "There is scarcely a more striking instance in American constitutional history of outright judicial disregard of congressional intent."[106]

When this decision was combined with *Santa Clara County v. Southern Pacific Rr Co.,*[107] where the Court unanimously ruled that the Fourteenth Amendment protects corporations as well as individuals, the door was opened for the judiciary to protect corporate interests. As a result, over the course of the next half-century, the Supreme Court established itself as the branch of government with an economic perspective. In fact, of the initial 554 Supreme Court decisions involving the equal protection clause, 426 were concerned with economic legislation (77%), while only 78 were concerned with racial discrimination

(14%).[108] This occurred despite the fact that Congress drafted the Fourteenth Amendment in order to protect blacks, not corporations.

With few exceptions, the Supreme Court maintained its role as the protector of corporate interests until the mid-1930s. It was then that President Franklin Delano Roosevelt, tired of the Court striking down his New Deal legislation as being unconstitutional, led a crusade against the Court in an attempt to force them to stop imposing their economic views on the will of the people. After these efforts eventually succeeded, the Court slowly began to change its focus from economics to civil liberties. It was after this time that the Bill of Rights finally came to the forefront of American constitutional debate.

Although in 1925 the Supreme Court made its astounding concession that the First Amendment freedoms of speech and press are applicable to the States[109] (thereby expanding the coverage of the Amendment enormously as well as the Court's powers to protect it), little else developed in terms of expanding the Bill of Rights protections to the States between the Civil War Amendments and the 1940s. For example, in 1914,[110] the Court applied the exclusionary rule for the first time. This rule forbids the use of illegally obtained evidence, in violation of the Fourth Amendment's unreasonable search and seizure restrictions, from being used against a defendant in court. In this case, the Court applied the rule only against federal agents. As a result, although federal courts were thereafter prohibited from using evidence illegally obtained by federal agents, if state agents or private individuals illegally secured evidence and handed it over to federal officers, it could then be used in a federal trial. This practice became known as the "silver platter doctrine" and was not prohibited by the Court until the 1960s.

During the 1930s, the Court began to support the notion that First Amendment liberties were superior to other civil liberties protections. In *Palko v. Connecticut*,[111] Justice Cardozo stated that they were on "a different plane of social and moral values," and that freedom of speech and thought is "the matrix, the indispensable condition, of nearly every other form of freedom....Neither liberty nor justice would exist if they were sacrificed." In *Murdock v. Pennsylvania*,[112] Justice Douglas stated that "Freedom of press, freedom of speech, freedom of religion are in a preferred position."

In the 1940s, the Supreme Court examined other First Amendment protections to see if they could be applied to the states. In *Cantwell v. Connecticut*,[113] the Court used the Fourteenth Amendment's guarantee of liberty, as found in the due process clause, to rule that the free exercise of religion clause of the First Amendment was applicable to the states. Since the freedom to practice one's religious convictions is on the same plane as free speech generally, the Court decided that it too was included within the concept of liberty protections the

Fourteenth Amendment demands states to observe. Seven years later, in *Everson v. Board of Education of Ewing Township*,[114] the Court ruled that the First Amendment clause prohibiting governmental establishment of religion was also binding upon the states.

But it was during the Warren Court era, between 1953 and 1969, that the Supreme Court exhibited a dramatic passion for protecting the rights of the individual. Chief Justice Earl Warren, the former Republican Governor of California, was persuaded to leave the governorship and become solicitor general on condition that he be nominated for the first vacancy on the court. After the death of Chief Justice Vinson, Warren was nominated to the Supreme Court by President Eisenhower. As a result of the makeup of the Court during his tenure as Chief Justice, at no time before or since has the individual been more important or respected in the eyes of the judiciary. From its landmark decisions on racial discrimination and legislative apportionment to its monumental rulings on criminal prosecution protections and privacy, this Court defined the notion of fundamental rights for American society.

Of all the decisions rendered by the Warren Court, none was more important than the series of cases decided in *Brown v. Board of Education*.[115] These cases addressed the issue of racial segregation in public education and the Court's decision would affect school systems within 21 states and the District of Columbia, involving some eight million white children and two and one-half million black children. Because of the importance of their decision, the Court was cautious in its approach. In fact, the Court had been unable to reach a decision when the case was first presented to it during the 1952 term. In scheduling the cases for reargument during the 1953 term, the Court submitted a lengthy list of questions to the attorneys concerning the intentions of the framers of the Fourteenth Amendment as well as requesting advice on the type of orders the Court should issue.

One concept that had to be addressed by the Court in *Brown* was the separate but equal doctrine. First announced by the Supreme Court in the 1896 case of *Plessy v. Ferguson*,[116] this decision provided states with a legal principle justifying policies which denied blacks their civil rights. As a result, Southern states almost immediately enacted laws segregating virtually every aspect of life, and blacks were systematically excluded from the political process and denied their fair share of public services, such as education. This discrimination continued well into the 20th century.

On 17 May 1954, Chief Justice Warren delivered the unanimous opinion of the Court. In ruling that segregation of the races was not permissible under the equal protection clause of the Fourteenth Amendment, Warren stated, "We conclude that in the field of public education the doctrine of 'separate but equal' has no place. Separate educational facilities are inherently unequal." Although the process of desegregating public schools took many years, this decision was monumental in its influence on how the country viewed the government's obligation to provide public services and protect the civil rights of all its citizens.

A second important issue addressed by the Warren Court was legislative districting, which involves the drawing of boundaries within states to determine representation in both state legislatures and the U.S. House of Representatives. Confronting the Court was its previous decision in *Colgrove v. Green*,[117] which told voters seeking relief from Illinois' malapportioned congressional districts to turn to their state legislature or Congress, not the courts. In ruling that this issue was a political question better dealt with by another branch of government, the Court stated that "it is hostile to a democratic system to involve the judiciary in the politics of the people."

When the Court reconsidered this issue in *Baker v. Carr*,[118] it was argued that, since a vote in a less populated district carries more weight than a vote in a more populated district, malapportionment is a violation of the equal protection clause. This time, the Court ruled malapportionment of state legislatures may constitute an equal protection violation and therefore federal courts have the power to provide a remedy. One year later, in *Gray v. Sanders*,[119] the Court laid down guidelines for how reapportionment may proceed by applying the one-person-one-vote principle. The reapportionment cases ended the practice of having districts with unequal populations throughout a state.

Protections for defendants in criminal trials were another major issue the Warren Court examined. In *Mapp v. Ohio*,[120] the Court applied the exclusionary rule to the states by stating, "having once recognized that the right to privacy embodied in the Fourth Amendment is enforceable against the states, and that the right to be secure against rude invasions of privacy by state officers is, therefore, constitutional in origin, we can no longer permit that right to remain an empty promise." In *Gideon v Wainwright*,[121] the Court ruled that the right to counsel, as protected by the Sixth Amendment, was fundamental and therefore required by the Constitution in all state felony prosecutions. In *Miranda v. Arizona*,[122] the Court combined the Fifth Amendment's protections against self-incrimination with the Sixth Amendment's provisions for right to counsel in setting up a stiff code of conduct for police interrogation. Generally, the Supreme Court has applied these criminal procedural protections to the states by way of the Fourteenth Amendment's liberty requirement within the due process clause.

Perhaps the most personal area of constitutional protection that the Warren Court developed was the concept of privacy. In *Griswold v. Connecticut*,[123] the

Court ruled that a state statute forbidding the use of contraceptives or advice as to their use interfered with "a right of privacy older than the Bill of Rights." Although not specifically mentioned in the Constitution, the justices separately pointed to a variety of sources supporting the guarantee of privacy. Justice Douglas found support in the "penumbra" of several fundamental constitutional guarantees, including the First, Third, Fourth, Fifth, and Ninth Amendments. Justices Harlan and White pointed to the *liberty* protections within the Fourteenth Amendment's due process clause, commonly referred to as substantive due process. Justice Goldberg stated that, since the Ninth Amendment "shows a belief of the Constitution's authors that fundamental rights exist that are not expressly enumerated in the first eight amendments," this supports his view that the due process clause of the Fourteenth Amendment protects all fundamental rights, including privacy. Regardless of where privacy comes from, this constitutional guarantee is now seen as one of the most important ones, and is zealously guarded by individuals.

Although freedom of speech protections had been extended to the states in the 1920s, due to the various limitations imposed on freedom of expression throughout the 20th century, this topic was something that clearly needed the Warren Court's attention. Whether it was the Court's initial attempts to articulate the clear and present danger test while reviewing violations of the Espionage Act of 1917 and Sedition Act of 1918[124]... or while reviewing violations of the various state criminal anarchy and syndicalism acts[125]... or while reviewing violations of the Smith Act (America's first federal peacetime restrictions on speaking and writing since the Sedition Act of 1798),[126] the Court could not seem to arrive at the proper balance between an individual's right to expression and a state's power to limit that expression. Finally, in 1969, after over half a century of balancing that right overwhelmingly in the favor of the state by criminalizing association, the Court articulated a test for free speech that protects the individual and has existed to this day. In *Brandenburg v. Ohio*,[127] the Court ruled that any advocacy falling short of a call for illegal action is wholly protected. In addition, speech calling for illegal action may also be protected as long as it is not being sought immediately, or there is reason to believe the listeners will refuse to commit the requested illegal action.

Other important decisions rendered by the Warren Court included: *New York Times v. Sullivan*[128] (where the Court enacted broad constitutional protection for freedom of comment); *Sherbert v. Verner*[129] (where the Court relaxed the harshness of the secular regulation rule by providing the availability of alternative means test for free exercise of religion cases); and *Duncan v.*

Louisiana [130] (where the Court ruled that defendants have a right to a jury trial in state criminal courts on the basis of the Fourteenth and Sixth Amendments).

Although the three chief justices to follow Earl Warren (Warren Burger, William Rehnquist, and John Roberts) have not displayed the same devotion to individual rights as Warren did, there have been some memorable developments during their tenures. For example, during the tenure of the Burger Court, *Roe v. Wade*[131] was decided. Justice Blackmun's opinion in this case stated that the right of privacy, although not an absolute right, was a fundamental right and therefore "broad enough to encompass a woman's decision whether or not to terminate her pregnancy." In addition, as a fundamental right, it can only be regulated by a compelling state interest "narrowly drawn to express only the legitimate state interests at stake." Blackmun conceded there were two legitimate state interests that could justify intervention: preservation and protection of the health of the pregnant mother and protection of the potentiality of human life, each of which "grows in substantiality as the woman approaches term and, at a point during pregnancy, each becomes compelling."

In addition, during this time the Court expanded the standard of review for equal protection cases by adding a middle tier. Since virtually all legislation involves classification, when reviewing a challenged classification within a statute, regulation, or policy, the Court generally applies the *rational basis test*. This test requires that any classification must be "*rationally* related to a *permissible* government interest" and provides states with a wide measure of discretion in developing classifications for legislation. Since the burden of proof (showing that the challenged classification is arbitrary) is placed upon the challenger, the Court's initial presumption is that the regulation is proper and the state usually wins under this level of scrutiny.

But if a law, regulation, or policy employs a *suspect classification* (such as race, national origin, religion, etc.) or *significantly burdens a fundamental right* (such as First Amendment rights, privacy, right to travel, etc.), then the Court examines that classification more closely by applying the *strict scrutiny test*. This test requires the classification to be "*necessarily* related to a *compelling* government interest" and the burden of proof is placed upon the government to show that it meets the test. Since the court's initial presumption under this level of scrutiny is that the regulation is improper, it is very difficult for a classification to pass this test (especially considering that even if the government can demonstrate the classification serves a compelling state interest, there also must not be a less burdensome alternative available for achieving the government's objective).

Finally, a third, intermediate standard of review (*quasi-suspect scrutiny*) was developed by the Burger Court to deal with gender and illegitimacy cases.

This test requires the classification to be *"substantially* related to an *important* government interest" and it places the presumption of regulatory constitutionality on equal footing. The result of these three tests has been that the Court requires greater legislative justifications for those classifications that are based on race, religion, gender, illegitimacy, or that significantly burden fundamental rights.

During the Rehnquist Court's tenure, a number of the precedents established by earlier courts were watered down. In *U.S v. Leon* [132] a facially-valid warrant was issued despite the fact that the officers presenting the affidavit for a search warrant had relied on information from both their own investigations and a confidential informant. After two lower courts ruled the police affidavit had not established probable cause because the information was stale and the informant's credibility had not been established, the Supreme Court modified the exclusionary rule by stating "so as not to bar the use in the prosecution's case-in-chief of evidence obtained by officers acting in reasonable reliance in a search warrant issued by a detached and neutral magistrate but ultimately found to be unsupported by probable cause." As a result, unless the affidavit is inadequate, or misleading (officer knows information is false or recklessly disregards its truth or falsity), or the judge is a "rubber-stamping" magistrate, or the warrant is facially deficient, as long as an officer reasonably relies on the warrant being properly issued, evidence gathered can be used at trial, even if the warrant is later shown to have been improperly issued.

In *Planned Parenthood of Southeastern Pennsylvania v. Casey*, [133] the Rehnquist Court overturned many of the important aspects of *Roe v. Wade*. Although the Court reaffirmed the central principle of Roe, the decision abandoned the trimester framework (because it "undervalues the state's interest in potential life" during the first two trimesters), articulated a new undue burden standard ("an undue burden exists, and therefore a provision of law is invalid, if its purpose or effect is to place a *substantial* obstacle in the path of a woman seeking an abortion before the fetus attains viability"), and upheld a number of state restrictions on abortion that would have been struck down under prior precedent (informed consent, parental consent, and recordkeeping provisions upheld). As a result of the Court's implication that any restrictions would no longer have to survive *strict scrutiny* analysis, states are freer to regulate abortion much more easily than before.

In *Adarand Constructors Inc. v. Pena*, [134] the Court reviewed a prime contractor's contract with the Department of Transportation that rewarded prime contractors with an additional payment for subcontracting with small businesses controlled by "socially and economically disadvantaged individuals". A subcontractor with a lower bid challenged the regulation claiming it discriminated on the basis of race and therefore violated the Fifth Amendment's equal protection "component." Ignoring the intentions of the framers of the Fourteenth Amendment and 1866 Civil Rights Act, as well as of those justices who developed strict scrutiny analysis (which were to protect the rights of those minority populations that have been historically discriminated against, particularly on the basis of race), the Rehnquist Court ruled "all racial classifications, imposed by whatever federal, state, or local governmental actor, must be analyzed by a reviewing court under strict scrutiny. In other words, such classifications are constitutional only if they are narrowly tailored measures that further compelling governmental interests." Whereas, prior to this line of cases,[135] only that legislation classifying on the basis of race that disadvantaged people belonging to a suspect class (race, national origin, gender, etc.) would be analyzed under strict scrutiny, after *Adarand*, all legislation classifying on the basis of race (whether in support of the historically disadvantaged or not) would now have to satisfy strict scrutiny analysis, a very difficult challenge.

Among the more recent decisions handed down by the Court are *Grutter v. Bollinger*[136] and *Gratz v. Bollinger*[137] (affirmative action in higher education cases involving the University of Michigan), and *Gonzales v. Carhart*[138] (addressing a federal prohibition of a specific abortion procedure). Whereas *Grutter* involved the graduate admissions policy at the university's law school, *Gratz* focused on the undergraduate admissions policy of the university's college of literature, science, and the arts. Although both were designed to promote racial diversity, the law school policy used race as a *factor* in order to obtain a *critical mass* of minority students, while the undergraduate policy was based upon a somewhat mechanical point system (that awarded minority applicants with additional points). Challenged as violations of the Fourteenth Amendment's equal protection clause and Title VI of the Civil Rights Act of 1964 (prohibiting racial discrimination in programs receiving federal financial assistance), the Court agreed race may be considered as a *factor* in achieving a diverse student body (upholding the law school policy), but disagreed that separate admission tracks for specific racial groups is constitutional (striking down the undergraduate policy). Instead, a "truly individualized consideration" in which race is merely one of the factors is what the constitution allows.

In *Gonzales*, the Roberts Court reviewed the constitutionality of the 2003 Partial Birth Abortion Act, a federal law similar to the Nebraska's ban on a late-term abortion procedure that had been struck down by the Court in 2000 (on the basis its wording was vague enough to impose an *undue burden* on legal abortions and it lacked a health exception for the mother). Despite the fact the 2003 federal legislation also lacked a health exception for the mother, the Court ruled this law did not place an *undue burden* on a woman's right to terminate her pregnancy because the wording was sufficiently specific and (deferring to the will of Congress) was not a procedure that is medically necessary. Interestingly, although Justice O'Connor had been a member of the majority striking down the Nebraska statute, her replacement on the Court (Justice Alito) had no similar concerns in upholding the federal law. As a result, *Gonzales* further supports the view, after *Casey*, that abortion rights are likely no longer fundamental (instead requiring intermediate scrutiny now) and state/federal legislatures have far more leeway in limiting abortions than at any time since *Roe v. Wade*.

The central reason for this dramatic shift in jurisprudential focus was the fact that, beginning over a quarter of a century ago, President Reagan began to apply an ideological litmus test to his nominations to the federal bench. Although presidents have always attached political priorities to their appointments, the extent to which Reagan did was monumental. Resurrecting the 19th century's focus on corporate interest protection (as well as its acceptance of conservative Darwinian political theory), and combining these with the University of Chicago's contemporary free-market, cost-benefit analysis philosophy, the Reagan Administration was able to appoint many proponents of this school of thought to different levels of the federal bench and various departments in his administration. Combining a pro-big business priority with a fondness for judicial activism, these administrators and judges have been able to shift bureaucratic and judicial policy away from civil liberties protections and towards corporate protectionism, states' rights, and law and order policies. As stated by Cass Sunstein, the highly respected University of Chicago law professor (who himself worked in the Reagan Justice Department during the 1980s), "...the contemporary federal courts are fundamentally different from the federal courts of two decades ago. The center has become the left. The right is now the center. The left no longer exists."[139]

Since the subsequent administrations of George H.W. Bush and George W. Bush have also embraced some of these philosophies, while opposing essential civil liberties protections, they have continued the Reagan policy of filling the federal bench with judicial conservatives. As a result, since Chief Justice Warren Burger's confirmation in 1969, 11 of the 14 justices nominated and confirmed to the Supreme Court have been republicans, with 7 of the current 9 justices on the Roberts Court being of that party.

Perhaps the most disturbing development over the course of the past few years has been the Supreme Court's general reluctance to review the constitutionality of the USA Patriot Act, the anti-terrorism law enacted by Congress in 2001 and modified and reauthorized in 2006. Despite the fact the

Court did rule the military commission authorized by the president to try detainees at Guantanamo was legally deficient in *Hamdan v. Rumsfeld*[140] (the commission procedures were below the requirements of both the Geneva Convention of 1949 and the Uniform Code of Military Justice), the Court has failed to examine the numerous provisions of the Patriot Act that lower the warrant requirements of judicial approval and/or dramatically expand the surveillance gathering powers of police agencies. Although the threat of terrorism is clearly a major problem and therefore should be a priority to government, so should the protection of precious civil liberties for which America has deservedly gained international acclaim over the past half century. Ignoring or watering down these sacred rights for millions of Americans, as a result of the actions of 19 terrorists, in essence disregards the efforts of countless individuals who have given their lives over the years in order to establish civil liberties.

In conclusion, it bears repeating the words Madison used when placing the proposed bill of rights amendment before the House of Representatives:

> If they are incorporated into the Constitution, independent tribunals of justice will consider themselves in a peculiar manner the guardians of those rights, they will be an impenetrable bulwark against every assumption of power in the legislative or executive; they will be naturally led to resist every encroachment upon rights expressly stipulated for in the constitution by the declaration of rights.[141]

---

[1] Schubert, Frank. INTRODUCTION TO LAW AND THE LEGAL SYSTEM, 9th Ed. (Houghton Mifflin, 2008) p.10.
[2] Schubert, *supra* n.1, p.10-11.
[3] Schubert, *supra* n.1, p.11.
[4] Banks, Christopher & O'Brien, David. COURTS AND JUDICIAL POLICYMAKING. (Pearson/PrenticeHall, 2008) p.8.
[5] Shapiro, Martin. COURTS: A COMPARATIVE AND POLITICAL ANALYSIS. (U. Chicago Press, 1981) p.79-80.
[6] Van Dervort, Thomas R. EQUAL JUSTICE: AN INTRODUCTION TO THE AMERICAN LAW AND THE LEGAL SYSTEM. (West, 1994) p.16.
[7] Calvi, James & Coleman, Susan. AMERICAN LAW AND LEGAL SYSTEMS, 6th Ed. (Pearson/PrenticeHall, 2008) p.30-31.

[8] Murphy, Walter & Pritchett, C. Herman. COURTS, JUDGES, AND POLITICS: AN INTRODUCTION TO THE JUDICIAL PROCESS, 4th Ed. (McGraw-Hill, 1986) p.9-10.

[9] Shapiro, *supra* n.5, p.100.

[10] Murphy & Pritchett, *supra* n.8, p.4.

[11] Van Dervort, *supra* n.6, p.18.

[12] Heuston, R.F.V. ESSAYS IN CONSTITUTIONAL LAW (Stevens & Sons, 1964) p.1.

[13] Dicey, Albert Venn. INTRODUCTION TO THE STUDY OF THE LAW OF THE CONSTITUTION, 10th Ed. (MacMillian, 1961) p.42. (quoting William Blackstone, 1 COMMENTARIES ON THE LAWS OF ENGLAND 160-61).

[14] Dicey, *supra* n.13, p.76-85.

[15] Dicey, *supra* n.13, p.40.

[16] Marshall, Geoffrey. CONSTITUTIONAL THEORY (Clarendon Press, 1971) p.1-2.

[17] Hobbes, Thomas. LEVIATHAN (1651).

[18] Mason, Alpheus & Baker, Gordon E., FREE GOVERNMENT IN THE MAKING: READINGS IN AMERICAN POLITICAL THOUGHT, 4th Ed. (Oxford U. Press, 1985), p.13.

[19] Mason & Baker, *supra* n.18, p.12.

[20] Mason & Baker, *supra* n.18, p.251-52.

[21] 5 U.S. (1 Cranch) 137 (1803).

[22] Murphy & Pritchett, *supra* n.8, p.481.

[23] Patricia W. Davies. *Smith Demands New Deal between People and State*, INDEPENDENT, March 2, 1993, p.6.

[24] Brazier, Rodney. CONSTITUTIONAL REFORM: RE-SHAPING THE BRITISH POLITICAL SYSTEM (Clarendon Press, 1991) p.128-29.

[25] *An Idea Whose Time Has Come*, CHARTER 88, March 1993, p.1, 3.

[26] Brazier, *supra* n.24, p.125.

[27] Dworkin, Ronald. A BILL OF RIGHTS FOR BRITAIN (Chatto & Windus, 1990) p.1-9, 16-17.

[28] Mr. Jack Straw, HANSARD, Volume 306, p.769 (16 February 1998).

[29] Straw, *supra* n.28, p.770.

[30] Mr. Kevin McNamara, HANSARD, Volume 306, p.801 (16 February 1998).

[31] Mr. Terry Davis, HANSARD, Volume 306, p.796 (16 February 1998).

[32] Straw, *supra* n.28, p.772.

[33] Mr. Paul Stinchcombe, HANSARD, Volume 306, p.815 (16 February 1998).

[34] Stinchcombe, *supra* n.33, p.816.

[35] Mr. Jack Straw, HANSARD, Volume 313, p.419-20 (3 June 1998).

[36] Sir Nicholas Lyell, HANSARD, Volume 306, p.852 (16 February 1998).

[37] Mr. Humfrey Malins, HANSARD, Volume 306, p.811-12 (16 February 1998).

[38] Sir Brian Mawhinney, HANSARD, Volume 306, p.784 (16 February 1998).

[39] Mawhinney, *supra* n.38, p.795.

[40] Hon. Geoffrey Palmer, A BILL OF RIGHTS FOR NEW ZEALAND: A WHITE PAPER 55 (Wellington, N.Z., Government Printer, 1985).

[41] Palmer, *supra* n.40, p.55-57.

[42] A.T.H. Smith, *The Human Rights Act 1998 (1) The Human Rights Act and the Criminal Lawyer: The Constitutional Context*, THE CRIMINAL LAW REVIEW 251, 259 (April 1999).

[43] *Constitutional Issues Facing the United Kingdom*, 30 L. LIBR. 13, 17 (1999).

[44] Human Rights Act, 1998, ch.42 (Eng.), reprinted in 7 HALSBURY'S STATUTES OF ENGLAND AND WALES 492-531 (Andrew Davies, et al. Eds., 4th ed. 1999).

[45] Robert Wintemute, *The Human Rights Act's First Five Years: Too Strong, Too Weak, Or Just Right?* 17 KCLJ 209-227 (2006) p.216.

[46] *A and others v. Secretary of State for the Home Department* [2004] UKHL 56.

[47] Wintemute, *supra* n.45, p.218.

[48] 18 June 2002, Application No. 63684/00.

[49] Wintemute, *supra* n.45, p.215 (footnote 24).

[50] British Institute of Human Rights, BRIEFING ON THE HRA, 16 May 2006, www.bihr.org, p.2-3.

[51] [2004] 3 All ER 411 (HL).

[52] Wintemute, *supra n.45,* p.212.

[53] BIHR, *supra* n.49, *Rachel Gunter (by her litigation friend and father Edwin Gunter) and Southwestern Staffordshire Primary Care Trust* [2005].

[54] Richard Clayton, The Human Rights Act Six Years On: Where Are We Now? 1 EUROPEAN HUMAN RIGHTS LAW REVIEW 11-26 (2007) p.25-26.

[55] Clayton, *supra* n.54, p.12.

[56] Williams, *supra* n.43.

[57] Walker, R.J., *The Treaty of Waitangi: as the Focus of Maori Protest*, WAITINGI:MAORI AND PAKEHA PERSPECTIVES OF THE TREATY OF WAITANGI, edited by I.H. Kawharu, 1989, p.263-64.

[58] Chief Judge Durie, *Protection of Minorities*, NEW ZEALAND LAW JOURNAL, 1987, p.260-61.

[59] Sir Robin Cooke, *Introduction*, NEW ZEALAND UNIVERSITITES LAW REVIEW, Vol.14, No.1, June 1990, p.1: "Some see it as a threat, and political capital is made out of that point of view; but in truth theirs is a tacit tribute to the Treaty, a reluctant recognition that it has become part of the essence of the national life. Even its critics have to accept that it is a foundation document. It is simply the most important document in New Zealand's history."

[60] Mulholland, R.D.. INTRODUCTION TO THE NEW ZELAND LEGAL SYSTEM (Butterworths, 1990) p.18, 23.

[61] Mulholland, *supra* n.60, p.29.

[62] Mulholland, *supra* n. 60, p.28-29.

[63] Dicey, *supra* n.13, p.202-3.

[64] Keith, K.J., *A Bill of Rights for New Zealand? Judicial Review versus Democracy*, A BILL OF RIGHTS FOR NEW ZEALAND, 1985, p.67-8.

[65] Keith, *supra* n.64, p.49.

[66] Human Rights Commission. A GUIDE TO THE PROPOSED BILL OF RIGHTS IN QUESTION AND ANSWER FORM, Wellington, N.Z., May, 1986, p.6: "New Zealand probably has fewer constitutional checks and balances than any other western democratic country. It is accordingly more vulnerable to abuses of executive and administrative power."

[67] Submission No. 140 to the Justice and Law Reform Committee on a Bill of Rights for New Zealand: A White Paper, New Zealand Law Society, p.5.

[68] *Bill of Rights Offers Only Limited Safeguards*, Speech to the Auckland Legal Foundation, HERALD, 7 March 1986.

[69] *Bill of Rights a Danger to Democracy*, NEW ZEALAND TIMES, 12 January 1986, p.10.

[70] FINAL REPORT OF THE JUSTICE AND LAW REFORM COMMITTEE ON A WHITE PAPER ON A BILL OF RIGHTS FOR NEW ZEALAND, New Zealand House of Representatives, 1988, p.3.

[71] MP Bill Dillon, HANSARD, Vol.510, p.3456.

[72] Minister of Justice W. P. Jeffries, HANSARD, Vol.509, p.2805.

[73] Prime Minister Geoffrey Palmer, HANSARD, Vol.510, p.3450.

[74] *Tugging on Superman's Cape: Lessons from Experience With the New Zealand Bill of Rights Act 1990*, PUBLIC LAW 266 [1998], p.274-75.

[75] [1992] 1 N.Z.L.R. 385 (Wellington C.A. 1991).

[76] [1992] 2 N.Z.L.R. 8 (Wellington C.A. 1991).

[77] 1991 BUTTERWORTHS CURRENT L. 2173 (Wellington C.A.).

[78] [1992] 3 N.Z.L.R. 260 (Wellington C.A.).

[79] [1994] 3 N.Z.L.R. 667.

[80] HANSARD, Vol.510, p.3449-50.

[81] [2004] 3 N.Z.L.R. 704.

[82] [2006] SC66/2005, NZSC62.

[83] Hogg, Peter W., *Canada's New Charter of Rights* (1984) 32 AMERICAN J. COMP. L., p.283: "Canada was formed in 1867 by the union of three of the British North American colonies. These colonies differed from the republic to the south in their loyalty to the British Crown. That loyalty manifested itself…in an acceptance by the Canadians of British political and constitutional values. Chief among these values was the 'sovereignty' of Parliament…"

[84] Hahn, Randolph, *Canada's Charter of Rights and Freedoms*, 1984 PUB. L. 530-31.

[85] *Robertson and Rosetanni v. The Queen*, 1963 S.C.R. 651, at p.654: "The Canadian Bill of Rights is not concerned with 'human rights and fundamental freedoms in the abstract sense but rather with such 'rights and freedoms' as they existed in Canada immediately before the Statute was enacted."

[86] Elman, Bruce P., *Altering the Judicial Mind and the Process of Constitution Making in Canada*, 28 ALTA. L. REV. 521 (1990), p.524.

[87] Beatty, David, *The Canadian Charter of Rights: Lessons and Laments*, 60 MODERN L.R. 481 (1997).

[88] *R. v. Oakes* (1986) 26 DLR (4th) 200.

[89] *R. v. Vaillancourt* (1987) 47 DLR (4th) 400.

[90] *Hunter v. Southam* (1984) 11 DLR (4th) 641; *R v. Therens* (1985) 18 DLR (4th) 655; *R v. Mannien* [1987] 1 SCR 1233.

[91] *Andrews v. Law Society of BC* (1989) 56 DLR (4th) 1; *Black v. Law Society of Alberta* (1989) 58 DLR (4th) 317.

[92] *Hunter…, supra* n.90.

[93] *Singh v. Minister of Employment and Immigration* (1985) 17 DLR (4th) 641.

[94] *R v. Big M Drug Mart* (1985) 18 DLR (4th) 321.

[95] *Supra* n.88.

[96] [1990] 3 SCR 697.

[97] [1999] 1 SCR 497.

[98] **(A)** Does the impugned law (a) draw a formal distinction between the claimant and others on the basis of one or more personal characteristics, or (b) fail to take into account the claimant's already disadvantaged position within Canadian society resulting in substantively differential treatment

between the claimant and others on the basis of one or more personal characteristics? **(B)** Is the claimant subject to differential treatment based on one or more enumerated and analogous grounds? and **(C)** Does the differential treatment discriminate, by imposing a burden upon or withholding a benefit from the claimant in a manner which reflects the stereotypical application of presumed group or personal characteristics, or which otherwise has the effect of perpetuating or promoting the view that the individual is less capable or worthy of recognition or value as a human being or as a member of Canadian society, equally deserving of concern, respect, and consideration?

[99] [1988] 2 SCR 712.

[100] For example, See: *Hunter v. Southam, supra* n.89, at pages 652-52; *R v. Oakes, supra* n.87, at pages 220-21; and *Retail et al v/ Dolphin Delivery LTD* (1986) 33 DLR (4th) 174, see p.184.

[101] *Supra* n.87, p.496.

[102] Cox, Archibald, THE COURT AND THE CONSTITUTION 38 (Houghton Mifflin, 1987).

[103] *Letter from Thomas Jefferson to James Madison* (Dec. 20, 1787) quoted in Alpheus Mason and Gordon E. Baker, eds., FREE GOVERNMENT IN THE MAKING: READINGS IN AMERICAN POLITICAL THOUGHT (Oxford. U. Press, 4th Ed., 1985) p.285: "Let me add that a bill of rights is what the people are entitled to against every government on earth, general or particular, and what no just government should refuse, or rest on inference."

[104] 7 Pet. 243 (1833).

[105] *Civil Rights Cases*, 109 U.S. 3 (1883).

[106] CONSTITUTIONAL CIVIL LIBERTIES (Prentice-Hall, 1984) P.252.

[107] 118 U.S. 394 (1886).

[108] Pritchett, *supra* n.106, p. 315.

[109] *Gitlow v. New York, 268 U.S. 652,* Justice Sanford stated: "We may and do assume that freedom of speech and of the press...are among the fundamental rights and 'liberties' protected...from impairment by the states."

[110] *Weeks v. U.S.*, 232 U.S. 383 (1914).

[111] 302 U.S. 319 (1937).

[112] 319 U.S. 105 (1943).

[113] 310 U.S. 296 (1940).

[114] 330 U.S. 1 (1947).

[115] 347 U.S. 483 (1954).

[116] 163 U.S. 537 (1896).

[117] 328 U.S. 549 (1946).

[118] 369 U.S. 186 (1962).

[119] 372 U.S. 368 (1963).

[120] 367 U.S. 643 (1961).

[121] 372 U.S. 335 (1963).

[122] 384 U.S. 436 (1966).

[123] 381 U.S. 479 (1965).

[124] *Schenck v. U.S.*, 249 U.S. 47 (1919); *Abrams v. U.S.*, 250 U.S. 616 (1919).

[125] *Gitlow v. New York*, 268 U.S. 652 (1925); *Whitney v. California*, 274 U.S. 357 (1927).

[126] *Dennis v. U.S.* 341 U.S. 494 (1951).

[127] *Brandenburg v. Ohio*, 395 U.S. 444 (1969).

[128] 376 U.S. 254 (1964).

[129] 374 U.S. 398 (1963).

[130] 391 U.S. 145 (1968).

[131] 410 U.S. 113 (1973).

[132] 468 U.S. 897 (1984).

[133] 505 U.S. 833 (1992).

[134] 515 U.S. 200 (1995).

[135] *Richmond v. J.A. Croson Co.* 488 U.S. 469 (1989); *Metro Broadcasting Inc v. FCC* 497 U.S. 547 (1990).

[136] 539 U.S. 306 (2003).

[137] 539 U.S. 244 (2003).

[138] 75 U.S.L.W 4210 (2007).

[139] *Fighting for the Supreme Court: How right-wing judges are transforming the Constitution,* HARPER'S MAGAZINE (September 2005) pp. 31-39, p. 34.

[140] 165 L. Ed. 2d 723 (2006).

[141] Mason & Baker, *supra* n.18, p.293.

Human Rights Act 1998
1998 Chapter 42
(Selected Provisions)

An act to give further effect to rights and freedoms guaranteed under the European Convention on Human Rights; to make provision with respect to holders if certain judicial offices who become judges of the European Court of Human Rights; and for connected purposes.   [9th November 1998] ...

Introduction

1. – (1) In this Act "the Convention rights" means the rights and fundamental freedoms set out in –
    (a) Articles 2 to 12 and 14 of the Convention,
    (b) Articles 1 to 3 of the First Protocol, and
    (c) Articles 1 and 2 of the Sixth Protocol,
    as read with Articles 16 to 18 of the Convention.

Legislation

3. – (1) So far as it is possible to do so, primary legislation and subordinate legislation must be read and given effect in a way which is compatible with the Convention rights.
    (2) This section –
    (a) applies to primary legislation and subordinate legislation whenever enacted;
    (b) does not affect the validity, continuing operation or enforcement of any incompatible primary legislation; and
    (c) does not affect the validity, continuing operation or enforcement of any incompatible subordinate legislation if (disregarding any possibility of revocation) primary legislation prevents removal of the incompatibility.
4. – (1) Subsection (2) applies in any proceedings in which a court determines whether a provision of primary legislation is compatible with a Convention right.
    (2) If the court is satisfied that the provision is incompatible with a Convention right, it may make a declaration of that incompatibility.
    (3) Subsection (4) applies in any proceedings in which a court determines whether a provision of subordinate legislation, made in the exercise of a

power conferred by primary legislation, is compatible with a Convention right.

(4) If the court is satisfied –

(a) that the provision is incompatible with a Convention right, and

(b) that (disregarding any possibility of revocation) the primary legislation concerned prevents removal of the incompatibility, it may make a declaration of that incompatibility.

Public Authorities

5. – (1) It is unlawful for a public authority to act in a way which is incompatible with a Convention right.

(3) In this section "public authority" includes –

(a) a court or tribunal, and

(b) any person certain of whose functions are functions of a public nature, but does not include either House of Parliament or a person exercising functions in connection with proceedings in Parliament.

8. – (1) In relation to any act (or proposed act) of a public authority which the court finds is (or would be) unlawful, it may grant such relief or remedy, or make such order, within its powers as it considers just and appropriate.

Remedial Action

10. – (2) If a Minister of the Crown considers that there are compelling reasons for proceeding under this section, he may by order make such amendments to the legislation as he considers necessary to remove the incompatibility.

Parliamentary Procedure

19. – (1) A Minister of the Crown in charge of a Bill in either House of Parliament must, before Second Reading of the Bill –

(a) make a statement to the effect that in his view the provisions of the Bill are compatible with the Convention rights ("a statement of compatibility"); or

(b) make a statement to the effect that although he is unable to make a statement of compatibility the government nevertheless wishes the House to proceed with the Bill.

SCHEDULES

Schedule 1
The Articles
Part I
The Convention

Rights and Freedoms

Article 2
Right to life

1. Everyone's right to life shall be protected by law. No one shall be deprived of his life intentionally save in the execution of a sentence of a court following his conviction of a crime for which this penalty is provided by law.

Article 3
Prohibition of torture

No one shall be subjected to torture or to inhuman or degrading treatment or punishment.

Article 5
Right to liberty and security

1. Everyone has the right to liberty and security of person. No one shall be deprived of his liberty save in the following cases and in accordance with a procedure prescribed by law:
   (a) the lawful detention of a person after conviction by a competent court;
   (b) the lawful arrest or detention of a person for non-compliance with the lawful order of a court or an order to secure the fulfillment of any obligation prescribed by law;
   (c) the lawful arrest or detention of a person effected for the purpose of bringing him before the competent legal authority on reasonable suspicion of having committed an offence or when it is reasonably considered necessary to prevent his committing an offence or fleeing after having done so;
   (d) the detention of a minor by lawful order for the purpose of educational supervision or his lawful detention for the purpose of bringing him before the competent legal authority;

(e) the lawful detention of persons for the prevention of the spreading of infectious diseases, of persons of unsound mind, alcoholics or drug addicts or vagrants;

(f) the lawful arrest or detention of a person to prevent his effecting an unauthorized entry into the country or of a person against whom action is being taken with a view to deportation or extradition.

2. Everyone who is arrested shall be informed promptly, in a language which he understands, of the reasons for his arrest and of an charge against him.

3. Everyone arrested or detained in accordance with the provisions of paragraph 1 (C) of this Article shall be brought promptly before a judge or other officer authorized by law to exercise judicial power and shall be entitled to trial within a reasonable time or to release pending trial. Release may be conditioned by guarantees to appear for trial.

4. Everyone who is deprived of his liberty by arrest or detention shall be entitled to take proceedings by which the lawfulness of his detention shall be decided speedily by a court and his release ordered if the detention is not lawful.

5. Everyone who has been the victim of arrest or detention in contravention of the provisions of this Article shall have an enforceable right to compensation.

Article 6
Right to a fair trial

1. In the determination of his civil rights and obligations or of any criminal charge against him, everyone is entitled to a fair and public hearing within a reasonable time by an independent and impartial tribunal established by law...

Article 8
Right to respect for private and family life

1. Everyone has the right to respect for his private and family life, his home and his correspondence....

Article 9
Freedom of thought, conscience and religion

1. Everyone has the right to freedom of thought, conscience and religion; this right includes freedom to change his religion or belief and freedom, either

alone or in community with others and in public or private, to manifest his religion or belief, in worship, teaching, practice and observance....

Article 10
Freedom of expression

1. Everyone has the right to freedom of expression. This right shall include freedom to hold opinions and to receive and impart information and ideas without interference by public authority and regardless of frontiers. This Article shall not prevent States from requiring the licensing of broadcasting, television or cinema enterprises...

Article 11
Freedom of assembly and association

1. Everyone has the right to freedom of peaceful assembly and to freedom of association with others, including the right to form and to join trade unions for the protection of his interests...

Article 14
Prohibition of discrimination

The enjoyment of the rights and freedoms set forth in this Convention shall be secured without discrimination on any ground such as sex, race, color, language, religion, political or other opinion, national or social origin, association with a national minority, property, birth or other status.

Part II
The First Protocol

Article 1
Protection of property

Every natural or legal person is entitled to the peaceful enjoyment of his possessions. No one shall be deprived of his possessions except in the public interest and subject to the conditions provided for by law and by the general principles of international law....

Part III
The Sixth Protocol

Article 1
Abolition of the death penalty

The death penalty shall be abolished. No one shall be condemned to such penalty or executed.

Article 2
Death penalty in time of war

A State may make provision in its law for the death penalty in respect of acts committed in time of war or of imminent threat of war: such penalty shall be applied only in the instances laid down in the law and in accordance with its provisions. The State shall communicate to the Secretary General of the Council of Europe the relevant provisions of that law.

New Zealand Bill of Rights Act 1990
(Selected Provisions)

An Act –
- (a) To affirm, protect, and promote human rights and fundamental freedoms in New Zealand; and
- (b) To affirm New Zealand's commitment to the International Covenant on Civil and Political Rights

BE IT ENACTED by the Parliament of New Zealand as follows:

PART I
General Provisions

2. Rights affirmed – The rights and freedoms contained in this Bill of Rights are affirmed.

3. Application – This Bill of Rights applies only to acts done-
- (a) By the legislative, executive, or judicial branches of the government of New Zealand; or
- (b) By any person or body in the performance of any public function, power, or duty conferred or imposed on that person or body by or pursuant to law.

4. Other enactments not affected – No court shall, in relation to any enactment (whether passed or made before or after the commencement of this Bill of Rights), -
- (a) Hold any provision of the enactment to be impliedly repealed or revoked, or to be in any way invalid or ineffective; or
- (b) Decline to apply any provision of the enactment –

by reason only that the provision is inconsistent with any provision of this Bill of Rights.

6. Interpretation consistent with Bill of Rights to be preferred – Wherever an enactment can be given a meaning that is consistent with the rights and freedoms contained in this Bill of Rights, that meaning shall be preferred to any other meaning.

PART II
Civil and Political Rights

Life and Security of Person

8. Right not to be deprived of life – No one shall be deprived of life except on such grounds as are established by law and are consistent with the principles of fundamental justice.

Democratic and Civil Rights

13. Freedom of thought, conscience, and religion – Everyone has the right to freedom of thought, conscience, religion, and belief, including the right to adopt and to hold opinions without interference.

14. Freedom of expression – Everyone has the right to freedom of expression, including the freedom to seek, receive, and impart information and opinions of any kind in any form.

16. Freedom of peaceful assembly – Everyone has the right to freedom of peaceful assembly.

17. Freedom of association – Everyone has the right to freedom of association.

Non-Discrimination and Minority Rights

19. Freedom from discrimination – (1) Everyone has the right to freedom from discrimination on the ground of colour, race, ethnic or national origins, sex, marital status, or religious or ethical beliefs.

   (2) Measures taken in good faith for the purpose of assisting or advancing persons or groups of persons disadvantaged because of colour, race, ethnic or national origins, sex, marital status, or religious or ethical belief do not constitute discrimination.

Search, Arrest, and Detention

21. Unreasonable search and seizure – Everyone has the right to be secure against unreasonable search or seizure, whether of the person, property, or correspondence or otherwise.

22. Liberty of the person – Everyone has the right not to be arbitrarily arrested or detained.

23. Rights of persons arrested or detained – (1) Everyone who is arrested or who is detained under any enactment –

(a) Shall be informed at the time of the arrest or detention of the reason for it; and

(b) Shall have the right to consult and instruct a lawyer without delay and to be informed of that right; and

(c) Shall have the right to have the validity of the arrest or detention determined without delay by way of *habeas corpus* and to be released if the arrest or detention is not lawful.

(2) Everyone who is arrested for an offence has the right to be charged promptly or to be released.

(3) Everyone who is arrested for an offence and is not released shall be brought as soon as possible before a court or competent tribunal.

(4) Everyone who is –

(a) Arrested; or

(b) Detained under any enactment –

for any offence or suspected offence shall have the right to refrain from making any statement and to be informed of that right.

(5) Everyone deprived of liberty shall be treated with humanity and with respect for the inherent dignity of the person.

24. Rights of persons charged – Everyone who is charged with an offence –

(a) Shall be informed promptly and in detail of the nature and cause of the charge; and

(b) Shall be released on reasonable terms and conditions unless there is just cause for continued detention; and

(c) Shall have the right to consult and instruct a lawyer; and

(d) Shall have the right to adequate time and facilities to prepare a defence; and

(e) Shall have the right except in the case of an offence under military law tried before a military tribunal, to the benefit of a trial by jury when the penalty for the offence is or includes imprisonment for more than 3 months; and

(f) Shall have the right to receive legal assistance without cost if the interests of justice so require and the person does not have sufficient means to provide for that assistance; and

(g) Shall have the right to have the free assistance of an interpreter if the person cannot understand or speak the language used in court.

25. Minimum standards of criminal procedure – Everyone who is charged with an offence has, in relation to the determination of the charge, the following minimum rights:

(a) The right to a fair and public hearing by an independent and impartial court:

(b) The right to be tried without undue delay:

(c) The right to be presumed innocent until proved guilty according to law:

(d) The right not to be compelled to be a witness or to confess guilt:

(e) The right to be present at the trial and to present a defence:

(f) The right to examine the witnesses for the prosecution and to obtain the attendance and examination of witness for the defence under the same conditions as the prosecution:

(g) The right, if convicted of an offence in respect of which the penalty has been varied between the commission of the offence and sentencing, to the benefit of the lesser penalty:

(h) The right, if convicted of the offence, to appeal according to law to a higher court against the conviction or against the sentence or against both:

(i) The right, in the case of a child, to be dealt with in a manner that takes account of the child's age.

27. Right to justice – (1) Every person has the right to the observance of the principles of natural justice by any tribunal or other public authority which has the power to make a determination in respect of that person's rights, obligations, or interests protected as recognized by law.

(2) Every person whose rights, obligations, or interests protected or recognised by law have been affected by a determination of any tribunal or other public authority has the right to apply, in accordance with law, for judicial review of that determination.

(3) Every person has the right to bring civil proceedings against, and to defend civil proceedings brought by, the Crown, and to have those proceedings

heard, according to law, in the same way as civil proceedings between individuals.

PART III
Miscellaneous Provisions

28. Other rights and freedoms not affected – An existing right or freedom shall not be held to be abrogated or restricted by reason only that the right or freedom is not included in this Bill of Rights or is included only in part.

CANADIAN CHARTER OF RIGHTS AND FREEDOMS
(Selected Provisions)

Whereas Canada is founded upon principles
that recognize the supremacy of God and the rule of law:

Guarantee of Rights and Freedoms

1. The Canadian Charter of Rights and Freedoms guarantees the rights and freedoms set out in it subject only to such reasonable limits prescribed by law as can be demonstrably justified in a free and democratic society.

Fundamental Freedoms

2. Everyone has the following fundamental freedoms:
   (a) freedom of conscience and religion;
   (b) freedom of thought, belief, opinion and expression, including freedom of the press and other media of communication;
   (c) freedom of peaceful assembly; and
   (d) freedom of association.

Democratic Rights...

Mobility Rights...

6. (4) Subsections (2) and (3) do not preclude any law, program or activity that has its object the amelioration in a province of conditions of individuals in that province who are socially or economically disadvantaged if the rate of employment in that province is below the rate of employment in Canada.

Legal Rights

7. Everyone has the right to life, liberty and security of the person and the right not to be deprived thereof except in accordance with the principles of fundamental justice.

8. Everyone has the right to be secure against unreasonable search or seizure.

9. Everyone has the right not to be arbitrarily detained or imprisoned.

10. Everyone has the right on arrest or detention
    (a) to be informed promptly of the reasons therefore;
    (b) to retain and instruct counsel without delay and to be informed of that right; and
    (c) to have the validity of the detention determined by way of *habeas corpus* and to be released if the detention is not lawful.

11. Any person charged with an offence has the right
    (a) to be informed without unreasonable delay of the specific offence;
    (b) to be tried within a reasonable time;
    (c) not to be compelled to be a witness in proceedings against that person in respect of the offence;
    (d) to be presumed innocent until proven guilty according to law in a fair and public hearing by an independent and impartial tribunal;
    (e) not to be denied reasonable bail without just cause;
    (f) except in the case of an offence under military law tried before a military tribunal, to the benefit of trial by jury where the maximum punishment for the offence is imprisonment for five years or a more severe punishment;
    (g) not to be found guilty on account of any act or omission unless, at the time of the act or omission, it constituted an offence under Canadian or international law or was criminal according to the general principles of law recognized by the community of nations;
    (h) if finally acquitted of the offence, not to be tried for it again and, if finally found guilty and punished for the offence, not to be tried or punished for it again; and
    (i) if found guilty of the offence and if the punishment for the offence has been varied between the time of commission and the time of sentencing, to the benefit of the lesser punishment.

12. Everyone has the right not to be subjected to any cruel and unusual treatment or punishment.

13. A witness who testifies in any proceedings has the right not to have any incriminating evidence so given used to incriminate that witness in any other proceedings, except in a prosecution for perjury or for the giving of contradictory evidence.

14. A party or witness in any proceedings who does not understand or speak the language in which the proceedings are conducted or who is deaf has the right to the assistance of an interpreter.

Equality Rights

15. (1) Every individual is equal before and under the law and has the right to the equal protection and equal benefit of the law without discrimination and, in particular, without discrimination based on race, national or ethnic origin, color, religion, sex, age or mental or physical disability.

     (2) Subsection (1) does not preclude any law, program or activity that has as its object the amelioration of conditions of disadvantaged individuals or groups including those that are disadvantaged because of race, national or ethnic origin, color, religion, sex, age or mental or physical disability.

Official Languages of Canada...

Minority Language Educational Rights...

Enforcement

24. (1) Anyone whose rights or freedoms, as guaranteed by this Charter, have been infringed or denied may apply to a court of competent jurisdiction to obtain such remedy as the court considers appropriate and just in the circumstances...

General...

Application of the Charter...

Citation...

THE UNITED STATES BILL OF RIGHTS

AMENDMENT I

Congress shall make no law respecting an establishment of religion, or prohibiting the free exercise thereof; or abridging the freedom of speech, or of the press; or the right of the people peaceably to assemble, and to petition the Government for a redress of grievances.

AMENDMENT II

A well regulated Militia, being necessary to the security of a free State, the right of the people to keep and bear Arms, shall not be infringed.

AMENDMENT III

No Soldier shall, in time of peace be quartered in any house, without the consent of the Owner, nor in time of war, but in a manner to be prescribed by law.

AMENDMENT IV

The right of the people to be secure in their persons, houses, papers, and effects, against unreasonable searches and seizures, shall not be violated, and no Warrants shall issue, but upon probable cause, supported by Oath or affirmation, and particularly describing the place to be searched, and the persons or things to be seized.

AMENDMENT V

No person shall be held to answer for a capital, or otherwise infamous crime, unless on a presentment or indictment of a Grand Jury, except in cases arising in the land or naval forces, or in the Militia, when in actual service in time of War or public danger; nor shall any person be subject for the same offense to be twice put in jeopardy of life or limb, nor shall be compelled in any criminal case to be a witness against himself, nor be deprived of life, liberty, or property, without due process of law; nor shall private property be taken for public use, without just compensation.

AMENDMENT VI

In all criminal prosecutions, the accused shall enjoy the right to a speedy and public trial, by an impartial jury of the State and district wherein the crime shall have been committed, which district shall have been previously ascertained by law, and to be informed of the nature and cause of the accusation; to be confronted with the witnesses against him; to have compulsory process for obtaining witnesses in his favor, and to have the Assistance of Counsel for his defence.

AMENDMENT VII

In suits at common law, where the value in controversy shall exceed twenty dollars, the right of trial by jury shall be preserved, and no fact tried by jury, shall be otherwise reexamined in any Court of the United States, than according to the rules of the common law.

AMENDMENT VIII

Excessive bail shall not be required, nor excessive fines imposed, nor cruel and unusual punishments inflicted.

AMENDMENT IX

The enumeration in the Constitution, of certain rights, shall not be construed to deny or disparage others retained by the people.

CHAPTER 3
THE HISTORY OF ROMAN LAW
AND THE DEVELOPMENT OF THE CIVIL LAW SYSTEM

Over the course of a millennium, Roman law evolved as a series of detailed and sophisticated rules that were developed by some of the greatest legal minds of the time. Beginning in the 6th century B.C., when Rome was merely a small community located on the Tiber River, the political nature of the city-state changed from a monarchy to a republic. Soon thereafter, concern rose on the part of the plebeians that their unwritten customs might be interpreted by the "college of pontiffs, a body of aristocrats responsible for maintaining the state religious cults,"[1] to advantage the noble propertied families. In response, a commission of ten citizens was appointed to prepare a written text of rules, based upon customary law. The resulting document became known as the *Twelve Tables* and it covered a broad spectrum of public and sacred law. Eventually, it was approved by the popular assembly of citizens and is now considered the beginning of Roman law.

Although the Greeks had spent a great deal of energy debating the nature and theory of law, the Romans were less concerned with philosophy. Instead, they were interested in developing rules governing property and legal proceedings. As a result, the *Twelve Tables* dealt mainly with the legal procedures necessary for the settling of disputes between citizens. Later, as the republic expanded, the control of legal remedies became the focus of Roman law, particularly for Roman citizens. At the same time, institutions were developed that were available to the ever-expanding numbers of non-citizens as well.

During this period, around the 3rd century B.C., mention "of a class of legal experts, jurists, who had no formal role to play in the administration of justice but who were prepared to explain the law"[2] began to emerge in the literature. Primarily concerned with private law, as opposed to religious, public, or criminal law matters, these late-republican jurists became the custodians of the law. Subsequently, the opinions of the more authoritative jurists were collected in works called *Digests*, for future reference on similar legal issues.

As the republic progressed into the last century B.C., a debate "between those who wanted to maintain the traditional constitution, even with its weakness of leadership, and those who wanted strong government, even at the cost of dispensing with the legal forms"[3] was being waged. Eventually, the Roman Empire replaced the republic and, despite the fact that some of history's greatest atrocities were committed in the name of emperors during this period, it was in these first two centuries of the Christian era that Roman law entered its classical period. Roman legal development was clearly at its most sophisticated level and the central reason for this progress was to be found in the vast amount of literature jurists were producing.

Yet, just as the 2nd century A.D. was perhaps the empire's most stable period, the subsequent century was just the opposite. By the end of the 3rd century A.D., the Roman Empire had spread far outside of Rome, and had to be divided into two regions, east and west. These regions in turn were divided into dioceses and prefectures. The 4th century found the eastern capital based in Constantinople, while the western capital was located in Milan. It was during this period, under the reigns of Constantine and Theodosius, that official persecution of Christians was finally prohibited and Catholicism became the official religion.

During the 5th century A.D. the grandsons of Theodosius, emperors of the western and eastern regions of the empire, approved the *Law of Citations* (426 A.D.) in an attempt to rectify the problem facing lawyers when conflicting writings on a specific issue were found. The *Law* made five of the most respected jurists in history (Papinian, Paul, Ulpian, Modestinus, and Gaius) the primary authorities to be relied upon when settling legal issues. The *Law* provided that the view of the majority prevailed if there was disagreement among the five authorities. If the views were equal in number, then Papinian's view was to be observed. "Only if the numbers were equal and Papinian was silent could the judge make up his own mind on the matter. The reduction of law-finding to a purely mechanical process is testimony to the fact that Roman legal science had reached its nadir."[4]

It was also during the 5th century (476 A.D.) that the western empire's last emperor gave up his throne and the west ceased to exist, leaving the ecclesiastical administration of the Church to attempt to assume some of the western empire's authority. As the Church was in the process of developing its own legal system, it put forward its view in a letter to the emperor of the eastern empire that there are two separate authorities in the world, the pope in spiritual matters and the emperor in temporal matters, with the Church retaining the right to try cases involving spiritual matters.

Although the western empire no longer existed, the second half of the fifth century saw legal scholarship and learning flourish in the eastern empire. It was into this environment that Justinian became emperor in 527 A.D. Justinian's ambitious goal was to return the eastern empire to the glory of its ancient past and restore Roman law to the levels achieved in its classical period, three centuries earlier. The first part of Justinian's goal to restore Roman law was achieved by putting the various imperial constitutions in chronological order in a *Code*, covering twelve books. In addition, as previously unresolved issues were discovered during this process, the new constitutions (*Novels*) of Justinian attempted to settle them for future legal reference.

"The most important part of Justinian's compilation was....the *Digest* (Latin *Digesta*; Greek *Pandectae*), an anthology of extracts from the writings of the great jurists."[5] In addition to including the five jurists cited in the *Law of Citations*, the *Digest* featured extracts from a number of other jurists, including some from the late republic. Since the *Code* and *Digest* were far too complex for beginning law students, Justinian ordered the publication of a new *Institutes*, an elementary textbook based on *The Institutes* by Gaius, which had originally been published in the middle of the 2nd century A.D. These three publications (The *Code*, *Digest*, and *Institutes*), all eventually became law and, in combination with subsequent constitutions (*Novels*) issued by Justinian, became known as *Corpus iuris civilis*. They reflected the culmination of a thousands years' legal development.

Beginning in the 6th century and lasting until the 11th, the central source for Roman law in the west was to be found in those kingdoms succeeding the empire that recognized the so-called barbarian codes, particularly the Visigothic kingdoms. Although not reflective of Roman law from the classical period, the law of the early middle ages essentially reflected various levels of Roman influence on Germanic customary laws. Only in parts of Italy, where Justinian's *Institutes*, much of the *Code*, and an abbreviated version of the *Novels* were known, was traditional Roman law understood. Perhaps the central figure in the maintenance of the Roman legal tradition was the Church. As the law of the Church developed, it increasingly faced complex issues that could more easily be dealt with by reference to the broad statements of principle announced in Roman law. As a result, "[m]uch of the canon law developed by the Catholic Church is based on Justinian's Codes..."[6]

It was during Western Europe's intellectual revival of the 12th and 13th centuries that "the creation of civil-law systems began."[7] During this period, renewed interest in the Justinian Code became evident, reference to Roman legal institutions was more prominent, ancient manuscripts began to be studied in 12th century Italian schools, and recovery of the entire *Corpus iuris civilis* was finally achieved. Yet, of all the manuscript discoveries, it was the rediscovery of the *Digest* that clearly was the most significant. Only through the study of this anthology of juristic writings on the law could students truly comprehend the science of Roman law.

"By the end of the twelfth century the position of Bologna as the legal centre (or 'mother of laws') of Europe was unchallenged and the *studium* had thousands of law students from all over Europe."[8] Thus, almost six centuries after Justinian had compiled the central writings of a thousand years of Roman legal thought, law as an academic discipline became the dominant subject of study. Both Roman and Canon (church) law, with its reliance on Roman law principles, became the major subjects in legal academia.

As news of the success that the University of Bologna was having in developing legal minds spread throughout Europe, schools began to imitate their teaching of Roman and Canon law, first in Italy and then elsewhere. Eventually, by the middle of the thirteenth century, those legal procedures derived from Roman law and later developed by Church courts began to be incorporated into secular court proceedings. Whether in England, where a number of the categories of Roman law were adopted in setting out the laws and customs of English common law in a Latin treatise known as *Bracton*; or in Spain, where the conclusion of Moorish domination led to the establishment of a center for canon and civil law at the University of Salamanca and the subsequent publishing of books of law (the *Siete partidas*) based on a combination of traditional customs, civil and canon law, and Old and New Testament rules; or in the Rhineland, where this Christian culture of Roman and Canon law was able to infiltrate lay and ecclesiastical positions of authority in lands that had never been included in the Roman empire;[9] Roman civil law laid a foundation for legal and political thought throughout the continent. This initial and elementary combination of substantive local rules with Roman law procedures marked the beginning of the adoption of Civil law.

The study of law in the 14th and 15th centuries was dominated by the Bartolus school of thought, named after the Italian doctor of law who wrote exhaustive commentaries on the *Corpus iuris civilis*. The central focus of this school was oriented towards finding solutions to contemporary problems. As this school of thought became more influential in training practitioners throughout Europe who were responding to current issues, it appeared civil law was moving further away from the law of Justinian. During this period, a new school of thought (Humanism) was evolving. As scholars who were passionate in their study of classical antiquity, humanists were skeptical of the authority, accuracy, and interpretations of *Corpus iuris* texts. "In their eyes, Tribonian, Justinian's minister in charge of the compilation, had not only excerpted the texts but in the process had mutilated them and introduced linguistic barbarisms."[10]

By the early 16th century, the humanist school of legal thought had spread from Italy to France, where it was enthusiastically accepted and studied at Bourges. At the heart of this movement was a desire to combine the rational, scientific structure of classical Roman law with contemporary substantive private law. In order to accomplish this, humanist scholars reconstructed the quality of the Roman texts. Thus, at the same time that reformers of the Church were critical of the authority and interpretations of Holy Scripture by Church Fathers, so too were the legal humanists critical of the diluted words of the texts relied upon by legal traditionalists.

It was also during this century that regional customs were increasingly being written down and codified in local communities. As professional courts were established to assume the more complex legal issues from local courts, many European states adopted a mixture of Roman-Canon legal procedures. The impact on the legal profession of this development was that civil lawyers became a powerful force in social and political life. At the same time, as legal scholarship had been the motivating force in the rediscovery of Roman law, university jurists (Doctors of Law) were held in high esteem in society and consulted regularly for their expertise and impartiality by courts of law.

In the 17th century, the universities in the Netherlands, particularly the school at Leyden, took the lead in the study of law much the way French universities had done in the sixteenth century and Italian universities before that. At the center of this development were Hugo Grotius, who published his famous treatise on international law (*De iure belli ac pacis*) while a political refugee in Paris, and Arnold Vinnius, a Leyden professor who combined elements of customary, Roman, and natural law to develop Dutch legal science. Although Grotius maintained international law was based on natural law and independent of civil law, his treatise makes numerous references to various texts of civil law in support of his natural law propositions. Vinnius, on the other hand, maintained that Roman civil law was the product of legal practice and universal laws emanating from nature.

It was during this century that university jurists began to recognize the need to comprehend local customary law, and not simply teach Roman civil law. As a result, books focusing on Roman-German law, Roman-Swedish law, and Roman-Dutch law were published that acknowledged the synthesis of Roman and local law.[11] At the same time, as the continent recovered from the ravages of decades of warfare, natural law was studied, debated, and offered as an alternative to the excesses of human emotions.

During the 18th century, political thought was dominated by the philosophy of the Enlightenment. Codification became the manner by which new rules could replace outdated ones, territories could be united within a state, judges could produce more consistent decisions, and commerce would benefit from uniform laws. Although, at the beginning of the century, Roman law held an eminent position in this evolution, by the end of the century it was generally seen as the outdated law of an expired society.

Over the course of the 19th century, a number of nations codified their national laws. Two of the most influential efforts were the codification movements of France and Germany. The French Civil Code attempted to replace all remnants of French aristocratic power with a simple, concise code reflecting the monumental concepts of natural justice (liberty, equality, and fraternity) expressed in the revolution. Developed during the reign of Napoleon, the code combines elements of both Roman and customary law into a law that is intended to prevent the abuses of power by nobility, clergy, and the judiciary that were so common in the 18th century. The French Civil Code soon became the model for other nations attempting to codify their laws, including Spain, Italy, Belgium, and the Netherlands.

The German Civil Code was not developed as a response to revolution; rather it was the product of a decades-long debate following the split of the Romanists and Germanists from the German Historical School. The Germanists were harsh critics of Roman law, arguing it was an alien law that was impeding the development of German law. The Romanists, led by Friedrich Karl von Savigny, countered that by examining the universal principles found in the original texts of Justinian and incorporating them into a code, German law could properly respond to the needs of a commercially oriented world. With its scientific approach to jurisprudence, the "German Civil Code of 1896 was a self-contained body of written law: Lawyers or judges did not have to resort to extraneous social, economic, political, or moral values to apply it."[12] Whereas the French Civil Code was the model for subsequent codes, German legal science became the dominant school of legal thought and made German law faculties the center of legal scholarship for Europe, much the way Italy, France, and the Netherlands had been in earlier centuries.

By the 20th century, although many European nations had codified their local laws so as to have a detailed body of rules by which lawyers and judges in their legal systems could logically resolve disputes, Roman law was no longer directly applicable in the courts of any major state. Despite this development, Roman law research and literature flourished throughout the century and its prominence on law faculties throughout Europe remains. At the same time, since "[a]scertaining and formulating these rules are primarily done by legal scholars in university settings rather than by courts and practitioners,"[13] the influence of and reliance upon academia in the civil law system has also flourished during this period, which is in somewhat stark contrast to the common law system.

Today, although "the model of the Civil Law is a code – a lucid, detailed, and all-encompassing set of interlocking regulations that ideally lay down in general principle, if not specific terms, the rules for settling all possible disputes among human beings,"[14] the reality is that no code can respond to changing circumstances quickly enough to meet such conditions. As a result, despite argument that the judge's main function is to simply discover the pertinent sections of the code and apply them without judicial creativity, the modern continental judge will invariably acknowledge the concepts, principles, doctrines, and conclusions established in prior cases during the course of his/her commentary and interpretation of the code. In some cases, particularly in Germany, specific discussions of prior cases will occur and their precedents will be acknowledged.[15]

One of the more interesting factors concerning the judicial system on the continent is that judicial service is a career path chosen during or soon after legal studies. Unlike a common law judge, who generally has been a practicing lawyer for a number of years before being named or elected to the bench, a civil law judge must choose between a number of options (civil service executive, governmental lawyer, private practice, or judge) early in his or her career and then begin life as a civil servant. This has resulted in far greater social contacts between the judicial and executive branches on the continent. Since promotion up through the ranks of the judiciary depends to some degree on conformity to bureaucratic priorities, judges are often seen as governmental officials, thereby inviting questions of judicial independence.[16]

Yet, it is in the separate and distinct area of administrative law that civil law judges seem to stand out. These special tribunals review the inter-agency, intra-agency, and agency-citizen relations of governmental administrative bodies in order to prevent administrative abuses. As a result of the prominence the bureaucracy holds in continental society, the ability of administrative judges to reign in arbitrary power has given them an excellent reputation in many nations.

One final characteristic of civil law systems is that they "employ an inquisitorial process of trial. The judge, rather than being a passive party, is an active participant in the trial. The judge's assigned task is to ascertain the truth, and the entire process revolves around him or her. The judge directs the investigation or the fact-gathering process. There are fewer technical rules of evidence and procedure, and trials are often rather informal, more closely resembling an administrative hearing than a full-blown trial."[17] When a case moves on to the appellate level, the initial appeals court can generally review questions of both fact and law. As a result, the court may decide to admit new evidence. In some circumstances the court may even choose to hold an entirely new trial. By the time the case reaches a continental state's highest appellate court (often called the *Court of Cassation*), many states prohibit that court from interpreting the facts. Instead, the court is simply permitted to examine the record for legal, procedural, and jurisdictional errors before remanding the case back to the lower appellate court level, for reconsideration in light of the higher court's instructions on the proper interpretation of the law. Thus, although the *Court of Cassation* is a court of last resort, in many states it is seen as a guardian of the proper interpretation of the Civil Code, rather than a court that makes the final judgment.

The French Constitution and Rights

With Charles de Gaulle providing the main impetus, the Constitution of the Fifth Republic was adopted on October 4, 1958, greatly expanding the powers of the president. In addition to establishing the nation as "an indivisible, secular, democratic and social Republic" and guaranteeing equality to all citizens regardless of origin, race, or religion,[18] the constitution stated the republic's motto "shall be Liberty, Equality, Fraternity"[19] and referred to the *Declaration of the Rights of Man and of the Citizen* in its Preamble. Yet, despite these references to important concepts of individual liberty, the constitution's provision for a Constitutional Council to possess the power to rule on the constitutionality of governmental bills was not originally seen as a major limitation on Parliament. In fact, since the only officials who could refer proposed legislation to the Council for constitutional review were generally members of the majority party or coalition, "[u]nder de Gaulle, the council was little more than a political joke. The one time it tried to assert its power, by finding his decision to hold a referendum on the direct election of the president unconstitutional, de Gaulle simply ignored its judgment and forged ahead."[20] Thus, with Parliament being given the constitutional discretion to enact specific laws concerning civil rights, fundamental public liberties, nationality, and criminal justice, and procedure,[21] the only real limitations on legislation over the course of the first decade or so were those imposed by Parliament itself.

Then, in 1971, the Constitutional Council (*Conseil Constitutionnel*) "gained great independence and prominence after it successfully asserted the right of judicial review"[22] and struck down a law on the basis it violated one of the principles mentioned in the *Declaration of the Rights of Man and of the Citizen*.[23] The court's decision was based on the logic that, since the *Declaration* is referenced in the Preamble of the constitution, and the constitution includes not only the document itself but also the principles emanating from the texts referenced in it, any law violating those principles contradicts the constitution and must be struck down. As a result of this case, it has been assumed that a number of texts are to be considered within the sphere of the constitution, including the Preamble to the 1946 constitution (which describes social rights and the equality of males and females) and the Charter for the Environment of 2004.

This case was evidence of the expanding role in government the judiciary has assumed over the course of the past few decades. Prior to the adoption of the Napoleonic Code, the judiciary had committed a variety of abuses as members of the French aristocracy. The codification of the laws was seen as an opportunity to eliminate the discretion of the courts by enacting detailed, comprehensive, and logical laws that a judge can easily apply to specific situations, thus eliminating the opportunity for the judicial independence sometimes seen in common law decisions. Consequently, the post-codification role of judges in society was reduced to one of little power or autonomy. Yet, despite this fact, the Council's assumption of judicial review in 1971, combined with a 1974 constitutional amendment (authorizing "opposition members of parliament to refer bills for review by the council"[24]), dramatically increased the powers of the Council to protect the constitution.[25]

As the *Declaration of the Rights of Man and of the Citizen* has become constitutionally relevant in France, it is important to understand both its historical evolution as well as its range of principles. The concepts included in the 1789 document are a product of the philosophy of the Enlightenment, as espoused by John Locke, Jean Jacques Rousseau, and Baron de Montesquieu. This fundamental document of the French Revolution lays down the foundation for France's shift from monarchy to republic, and declares natural rights, not the divine right of kings, as the basis for law in society. Among the rights mentioned are the natural rights of "liberty, property, security, and resistance to oppression"; popular sovereignty; equality of opportunity; the freedoms of speech, press, and religion; the presumption of innocence until declared guilty; and the prohibition of *ex post facto* laws. These concepts stood in stark contrast to the pre-revolutionary era's celebration of society's aristocracy and the clergy.

Yet, although the French *Declaration* (like the American *Declaration of Independence* before it) professed allegiance to a number of noble principles, there were entire segments of the population who were generally left out of its provisions. Among them were women, who had to wait until the 20th century for equal protection at the national level in both nations, and those people suffering from the institution of slavery.

Despite the fact the Constitutional Council is the only court with the power of judicial review (the power to invalidate a law inconsistent with the French Constitution), there are two other courts of last resort that are also extremely important in the French legal system. The Court of Cassation (*Cour de Cassation*) is the highest court in France and it possesses the power to affirm or reverse lower court judgments in any of the six different chambers of French courts, covering issues ranging from individual rights, to contracts and property disputes, as well as to corporate, criminal, or labor law. Even though the concept of *stare decisis* is not followed in France, there is a doctrine known as *jurisprudence constante* that encourages judges to follow the decisions of higher courts. As a result, decisions of the Court of Cassation can have the effect of fundamentally changing the interpretation of laws in the civil code.

The second court of last resort that possesses a special importance to the protection of rights is the State Council (*Conseil d'Etat*). Besides advising the government on the legality and constitutionality of proposed regulations, the State Council stands as the final step in the hierarchy of France's expansive administrative court system. Seen as a "watchdog on the executive.....in the French political system, where the executive has such great autonomy,"[26] the Council reviews allegations of individual rights violations against administrative bodies and has the power to fashion appropriate remedies.

Since the Constitution of the Fifth Republic went into effect, Parliament has enacted a great number of laws dealing with civil rights, fundamental public liberties, and criminal law and procedure. As discussed previously, in addition to the various state courts available to protect rights and liberties, continental states also have the benefit of an additional level of judicial review, that being the European Court of Human Rights. In 2003, France was one of four states accounting for 60% of all the ECHR judgments, while in 2004, France was one of four states accounting for 50% of all the ECHR judgments. *Saoud v. France*,[27] *Frerot v. France*,[28] *Tais v. France*,[29] and *Dupuis and Others v. France*[30] are among the recent decisions announced by the European Court of Human Rights involving France.

Saoud v. France involved the death of a French/Tunisian national, Mohamed Saoud, while in the custody of police officers. During the process of responding to a call concerning a disturbance, police found Saoud assaulting his mother and two sisters. One of the sisters informed the police that her brother was suffering from schizophrenia and was recognized as 80% disabled, and that a physician needed to be called. Rather than calling for a physician, police eventually took Saoud into custody but not before the process turned violent and both a number of officers and Saoud were injured. After being subdued and handcuffed, various police officers continued to hold Saoud to the ground for 35 minutes, which resulted in his dying of gradual asphyxiation. Although officers were treated for their injuries, Saoud did not receive a medical exam. After the case had proceeded through the French state courts, the ECHR ruled unanimously that French authorities violated Article 2 of the *Convention* (right to life) by not fulfilling their obligation to protect the life of Mohamed Saoud, as well as Article 6.1 (right to a fair hearing) because it was materially impossible for the lawyer subsequently assigned to present the appeal to the Court of Cassation to file proceedings in a timely manner.[31]

In 1986, the Minister of Justice issued circulars allowing strip searches and prohibition of communications in prisons. Maxim Frerot, a French national serving life imprisonment, filed an administrative appeal in 1994 requesting annulment of the provisions on the basis that, first, the searches would result in the probability of force, and second, the prohibition of correspondence was censorship. Upon review, the ECHR unanimously ruled in *Frerot v. France* that authorities violated Article 3 of the *Convention* (prohibition of degrading treatment), Article 8 (right to respect for correspondence), Article 13 (right to an effective remedy), and Article 6.1 (right to a fair trial within a reasonable time). Although the court found strip searches to be appropriate in certain circumstances, the level of discretion afforded prisons in France and the number of strip searches imposed on Frerot in one of the prisons amounted to inhuman and degrading treatment.[32]

Tais v. France involved the death of a French national, Pascal Tais, while in the custody of police. After being involved in a minor road accident, Tais and his girlfriend were stopped and questioned by police, which resulted in a fight. They were then taken to a hospital for a medical exam, whereupon Tais refused and was subsequently struck repeatedly to the hands, legs, and chest by police with batons. After being checked by a physician (who observed he was somewhat inebriated) and released from the hospital, Tais was placed into an overnight cell to sober up. Although the custody report states officers checked on him 23 times during the early morning hours, Tais was found dead in his cell at 7:30am, lying in a pool of blood and excrement. While an autopsy ruled his death was the result of hemorrhaging due to a rupture of the spleen, the Indictments Division of the Bordeaux Court of Appeal upheld the lower court's ruling that there was no case to answer as to the custodial officers and that the cause of death probably occurred while Tais was sobering up and fell. The ECHR ruled 5-2 that the French authorities violated Article 2 of the *Convention* (right to life) as to the death of Tais, and then ruled unanimously that they also violated Article 2 in their lack of an effective investigation into the circumstances surrounding his death.

The Court stated that persons in custody are in a vulnerable position: therefore, authorities are under a duty to account for their treatment of them. In this instance, the injuries reported in the hospital exam of Tais differed from the injuries found in his autopsy, including many recent bruises, injuries to his scalp, and two broken ribs. Since Tais was in an extremely fragile state, due to AIDS, his condition was exacerbated by the police blows. As such, it is incumbent on authorities to provide a plausible explanation as to the events leading to his death.[33]

The book *The Ears of the President* (*Les Oreilles du President*) was written by two French journalists, Jerome Dupuis and Jean-Marie Pentant, and published in 1996. It examined the illegal system of governmental phone tapping and record keeping operated by the French anti-terrorism unit within the French President's Office between 1983 and 1986, and which was referred to as the "Elysee eavesdropping" operations. In 1993, a judicial investigation for breach of privacy was initiated against the Deputy Director of President Mitterand's private office during the time in question. After the book came out, the former deputy director lodged a complaint against the journalists claiming some of the book's facts were based upon information included in the judicial investigation's confidential file. The journalists were eventually convicted and fined for using and reproducing material from a pending criminal investigation for their book. Upon review, the ECHR ruled unanimously that authorities violated Article 10 of the *Convention* (freedom of expression) on the basis that the public had a legitimate interest in the surveillance operation examined in the book, the information in the book contributed to the public debate on the matter, and (since some of the confidential information was already made public during the investigatory process) the importance of confidentiality during a judicial investigation does not override the freedom of expression requirement.[34]

The German Constitution and Rights

The Basic Law for the Federal Republic of Germany (*Grundgesetz fur die Bundesrepublik Deutschland*) came into effect in 1949. "Under Allied guidance during the occupation, the builders of the postwar government sought to inhibit centralized power by establishing a federal system with significant powers for the states (*Lander*). It is paradoxical that a document that owes so much to the influence of foreign powers has proved so durable. Under the Basic Law of the Federal Republic, many functions that had formerly been centralized during the imperial, Weimar, or Nazi periods, such as the educational system, the police, and the radio networks, now became the responsibility of the states."[35]

Whereas under the Weimar Constitution, rights were somewhat seen as state objectives, the Basic Law guarantees certain rights as fundamental. Among the various rights provided for in the Basic Law are: "Human dignity shall be inviolable",[36] "Every person shall have the right to life and physical integrity",[37] "Men and women shall have equal rights",[38] the freedoms of religion, expression, assembly, and association,[39] privacy of correspondence,[40] the inviolability of the home,[41] and the right of asylum.[42] As a result, "the Basic Law contains a more elaborate and explicit statement of individual rights than exists in either the U.S. Constitution or in the British Common Law."[43]

Similar to the French system, the judiciary in Germany relies upon a comprehensive, detailed code, partially based in theory on Roman law and the Napoleonic code. As with other civil law nations, German judges are much more active in the administration of the laws and implementation of their societal and political goals than are Common law judges. Whereas, in the United States, judges who set policy are sometimes criticized for trying to legislate from the bench, it is expected that German judges have a role in shaping policy.

The German court system is composed of three main branches. The first branch contains the various levels of courts dealing with general criminal and civil matters. The highest court in this branch is the Federal Court of Justice (*Bundesgerichtshof*) and it reviews appeals from the lower state courts in an attempt to provide judicial consistency and predictability throughout the 16 states. The second branch contains the specialized courts examining issues concerning administrative, tax, social security, patent, and labor law. Like the ordinary courts dealing with criminal and civil matters, these courts are organized in a federal/state hierarchy beneath a federal appeals court. Although the jurisdiction of this branch is somewhat narrow, because the state and its bureaucracy play such a fundamental role in the everyday life of German citizens (including safety standards, working conditions, collective bargaining agreements, unemployment compensation, social security payments, tax issues, and industrial property rights), these specialized courts provide a necessary check on any arbitrary decision-making by the bureaucracy.

The German Federal Constitutional Court (*Bundesverfassungsgericht*) is the highest court in the third branch in the German court system, the constitutional courts. Possessing the power of judicial review over the constitutionality of laws, this court "is regarded and known as the 'Huter der Verfassung' (guardian of the constitution). Its rulings are binding for all constitutional organs of the Federation and the *Lander* just as for all courts and public authorities."[44] Unlike the French

Constitutional Council (where the court may only review and invalidate an unconstitutional law before it is promulgated), as guardian of the constitution, the German Federal Constitutional Court is competent to review the constitutionality of a much broader array of laws and procedures. Constitutional cases may be initiated from a number of sources, including: the federal government, regional government, or one third of the parliamentary members of the *Bundestag* concerned with the constitutionality of a federal or regional law; regular courts concerned with the constitutionality of a particular law; the federal or regional government disputing the rights and duties between the Lander and the Federation; or individual citizens alleging their fundamental rights have been violated. "Initially authorized by statute, this provision became so important that in 1969 the Basic Law was amended to constitutionalize the right (of individuals) to file constitutional complaints."[45]

Over the course of the past few years, the European Court of Human Rights has ruled on a number of important cases involving Germany. *Jorgic v. Germany*,[46] *Jalloh v. Germany*,[47] *Epple v. Germany*,[48] and *Storck v. Germany*[49] are a few of these cases the court has recently decided. Nicola Jorgic, a national of Bosnia and Herzogovina, was a legal resident of Germany from 1969 to 1992. Of Serb origin, Jorgic returned to his birthplace in 1992. Upon his return to Germany in 1995, he was arrested and placed in pretrial detention on the grounds he was suspected of committing acts of genocide during the 1992 period of ethnic cleansing in his homeland. Facing allegations of organizing a paramilitary group that assaulted and killed Muslim men and women, as well as elderly and disabled Muslims in a number of villages, Jorgic challenged Germany's jurisdiction to try him. He was subsequently convicted and sentenced to life imprisonment by a German Court of Appeal claiming to possess jurisdiction in accordance with the state's humanitarian and military missions in the region, the applicant's residence in Germany for over twenty years and the fact he was arrested there, as well as the fact there are no public international law prohibitions to their trying the case. In reviewing the complaint, the ECHR ruled unanimously there was no violation of Article 6.1 (right to trial), Article 5.1 (right to liberty and security), or Article 7 (no punishment without law) of the European Convention. The Court stated that Germany's interpretation of the Article VI of the Genocide Convention, in light of Article I of that Convention, was supported widely by statutory provisions and caselaw. Therefore, trying Jorgic in a tribunal established by law on charges of genocide was reasonable, not arbitrary. Likewise, as Jorgic was lawfully detained after his conviction by a competent court, there was no violation of Article 5.1. Finally, as to Article 7, since there are conflicting views among courts as to what entails the crime of genocide, Germany is entitled to determine which interpretation they choose to adopt.[50]

Abu Jalloh, a national of Sierra Leone living in Cologne, was seen by police pulling two small plastic bags out of his mouth and exchanging them for money. As they were attempting to arrest Jalloh for suspected drug dealing, he swallowed another bag he still had in his mouth. A public prosecutor then ordered Jalloh be given an emetic to force him to regurgitate the bag. After he refused to take the medication at the hospital, four officers held him down as a physician inserted a tube through his nose and administered medication. Eventually, Jalloh regurgitated a small bag containing 0.2182 grams of cocaine and was convicted. After appealing unsuccessfully in the German courts, Jalloh filed a complaint based on the European Convention. The ECHR ruled 10-7 that there was a violation of Article 3 (prohibition of inhuman and degrading treatment) and 11-6 that there was a violation of Article 6.1 (right to fair trial). As for Article 3, the court ruled that, although the *Convention* did not prohibit recourse to forcible medical intervention in support of a criminal investigation, any interference with physical integrity for the purposes of obtaining evidence would be subject to the most rigorous scrutiny. In this instance (despite the fact the procedure was administered in a hospital by a physician) Jalloh's violent reaction and resistance to the procedure, his inability to speak German, as well as his being forcibly restrained and observed during the waiting period after the procedure, all contributed to additional health risks and humiliation for the applicant, especially considering the fact the authorities could have simply waited for the drugs to pass out of his body naturally. As for Article 6.1, the court stated that the administration of this procedure, combined with the fact the evidence collected was the decisive factor in securing Jalloh's conviction, breached a core right guaranteed in the *Convention* by infringing on his right not to incriminate himself.[51]

In *Epple v. Germany*, Ulrich Epple, a German national attending a Chaos Day folk festival on the island of Lindau, was approached by police and asked to leave the site of the festival. When he refused, they told him to leave the island for the remainder of the weekend. After he failed to comply, police checked their data banks and discovered Epple had attended previous festivals and arrested him. He was then taken into custody and detained in the police station until 1:45pm the following day. Epple challenged his arrest and detention on the basis police were discriminating against him because of his punk-like appearance, which violated his Article 10 (freedom of expression), Article 14 (prohibition of discrimination), and Article 5 (right to liberty and security) rights. The ECHR declared the Article 5 complaint was the only applicable one. Although the court stated Epple's arrest and initial detention did not violate Article 5.1, when his length of time in custody was combined with the judge's delay in considering the case the following day, the court ruled Epple's right to liberty was violated.[52]

Waltraud Storck, a German national, was placed in a private psychiatric clinic in 1977 at her father's request, despite the fact the applicant had already reached the age of majority, she had not been placed under anyone's guardianship, she had never signed a consent declaration to being placed in an institution, and no judicial officer had authorized her detention in a psychiatric clinic. During her 1977-79 stay in the private hospital, Waltraud repeatedly tried to flee the clinic. One time, in March of 1979, she was forcibly brought back to the clinic by police. Later, after receiving treatment for schizophrenia, she developed post-poliomyelitis syndrome and became 100% disabled, even losing the ability to speak for a number of years. In 1994, it was discovered and reported by experts that she had never suffered from schizophrenia. Instead, her behavior was simply caused by her family conflicts. In 1997, Waltraud filed an action against the private clinic for damages. Although the Regional Court allowed the action for illegal detention, the Court of Appeal quashed the judgment and dismissed the claim on the basis it was time-barred. After the Federal Court of Justice refused to admit the appeal, and the Federal Constitutional Court refused to admit the complaint, the ECHR ruled the German authorities violated Article 5.1 (right to liberty and security) and Article 8 (respect for private and family life). The court stated that (since there was no judicial authorization for the detention and it was obvious the applicant did not wish to stay in the clinic) Germany's active participation in forcibly bringing her back to the clinic after she had fled, the national courts' failure to properly interpret their civil law provisions within the spirit of Article 5, and Germany's failure to meet the state's ongoing obligation to protect Waltraud against interferences with her liberty by private actors, resulted in Germany being held responsible for the violation of Article 5 *Convention* rights. As Germany was likewise responsible for her medical treatment, Article 8 was also violated.[53]

The Italian Constitution and Rights

The Constitution of the Italian Republic (*Costituzione della Repubblica Italiana*) became law on January 1, 1948. Originally composed of 139 articles, the Constitution is organized into three main sections: The Fundamental Principles (*Principi Fondamentali*), Rights and Duties of Citizens (*Diritti e Doveri dei Cittadini*), and Organization of the Republic (*Ordinamento della Repubblica*), followed up by a number of Transitory and Final Provisions. Although Articles 13-28 may be similar to the bills of rights found in some Common Law states, there are a number of important individual rights protected elsewhere in the document as well.

Among the various civil liberties included in the document are: equality before the law and equal access to the political, economic, and social organization of the country;[54] a prohibition against unreasonable search or seizure of person [55] or of personal domicile;[56] the freedoms of correspondence,[57] movement,[58] association,[59] religion,[60] and speech and press;[61] the obligation of government to provide free medical care to the poor;[62] equal rights and comparable pay for women;[63] and the guarantee of adequate insurance for workers "in case of accident, illness, disability, old age, and involuntary unemployment."[64]

Italy adopted a codified system, with both French and German influences. While the Italian Code is closer in style to the French Code, the dominant role of the law professor in the Italian system goes beyond that of both the legal academic in France and Germany. This is probably due to the fact that, whereas the French Code was a legislative creation, as compared to the greater academic influences in the German Code, legal academics in Italy created the *Doctrine* (which is a foundational source for legal academia, statutory interpretation, and judicial decisions).[65]

The Supreme Court of Cassation (*Corte Suprema di Cassazione*) is Italy's general court of last resort. The court is divided up into various sections dealing with different types of law, such as criminal or civil, but its central role is to ensure the correct interpretation of law throughout all the inferior and appellate courts. Although the Supreme Court may not rule on the constitutionality of laws or review a lower court's interpretation of the evidence, it can correct a lower court's interpretation of law, jurisdiction, or legal process by invalidating it and stating the correct legal interpretation.

The Constitutional Court of Italy (*Corte costituzionale della Repubblica Italiana*) is the other court of last resort. The Constitutional Court can rule on the constitutional validity of "laws and enactments having the force of law," pass judgment on conflicts between regions or between the state and regions, and rule on the constitutional legitimacy of accusations made against the president of the republic.[66] Once a law is ruled unconstitutional and that decision is published, "the law ceases to have effect."[67] A decision by the Constitutional Court can not be appealed.[68]

Like France, Italy has been a frequent party in ECHR judgments. Italy was one of four states accounting for over 60% of the court's judgments in 2003 and over 50% of the judgments in 2004. In 2005, it was one of five states accounting for over 60% of all ECHR judgments. *Ormanni v. Italy,*[69] *Graviano v. Italy,*[70] *Maestri v. Italy,*[71] and *L.M. v. Italy*[72] are a few of the more recent decisions handed down by the court involving Italy.

Roberto Ormanni, an Italian national, was a magazine journalist. One of his published articles detailed an interview with a dance academy's principal dancer, who alleged his recent criminal charges for rape were actually the result of a conspiracy by a local business committee seeking to do him harm. In addition, the dancer alleged he had lodged a complaint about a theft at the academy with the local prosecution service but that, as the head of the service was the brother-in-law to the manager of the rival dance academy, the service had decided to take no further action. Although the magazine allowed the head of the prosecution service the opportunity to present his version in the following edition, he still lodged a complaint against the journalist and principal dancer, alleging defamation through the medium of the press. The Court of Appeal found both defendants guilty and the Court of Cassation declared their appeals inadmissible. Upon review, the ECHR ruled that, although the article contained a degree of provocation, it could not be considered a gratuitous personal attack on the head of the prosecution service. Besides the fact that the magazine gave the head of the service an opportunity to present his own version in the next edition, the dancer's remarks were legitimate issues for the press to inform the public about since they covered a subject of general interest (possible links between politicians, private interests, and judicial institutions). As a result, the court found authorities had violated Article 10 of the *Convention* (freedom of expression).[73]

Guiseppe Graviano, an Italian national, was charged with murder and membership in a mafia-type organization. During his trial, one of the eight judges was transferred to other duties and replaced after witnesses had been questioned. Graviano objected to the inclusion in the judges' files the records of all the witness examinations before the change, as well as to the fact the court refused to have the witness examinations repeated. He was subsequently convicted and sentenced to life imprisonment. The Court of Appeal and Court of Cassation refused requests to have witnesses examined again. Although the ECHR observed the fact that a change in judicial composition after witness examination normally requires re-examination of the witnesses, the circumstances in this case justified an exception to the rule. Since the applicant had not been deprived of his right to question the witnesses and there was no indication re-examination would have resulted in any new evidence being presented, there was no infringement on the applicant's right to due process, particularly since the new judge was able to read the hearing reports and the other seven judges had all been present during initial examinations. As such, the court ruled unanimously there was no violation of Article 6.1 or 6.3(d) (right to a fair hearing).[74]

Angelo Massimo Maestri, an Italian national and judge, was acting president of the La Spezia District Court. After disciplinary proceedings were brought against him for being a member of the Masonic Lodge (on the basis it is incompatible for a judge to properly administer his or her judicial oath after they have also taken the Masonic oath), the National Council of the Judiciary found Maestri had committed the offenses charged against him and reprimanded him. In reviewing the complaint, the ECHR did find the disciplinary measure had a basis in Italian law (Article 18 of the Royal Legislative Decree of 31 May 1946 and the National Council of the Judiciary directives of 1990 and 1993 all prohibited judges from joining the organization). However, as Article 18 did not define how a judge could exercise his or her freedom of association in light of the prohibition, and the 1990 directive only prohibited judges from joining certain proscribed associations (as opposed to requiring judges to resign from any prior memberships), neither regulation satisfied the condition of foreseeability required of a law since it was unclear Maestri's membership (which lasted from 1981 to 1993) could result in sanctions. Thus the court ruled the Italian authorities violated Article 11 (freedom of assembly and association) of the *Convention*.[75]

In *L.M. v. Italy*, applicant is an Italian national who had her home searched in connection with the suspected offense of unlawful possession of firearms. The suspected offender was applicant's son, who lived with her and had previously run afoul of the law. The search resulted in no unlawful objects being found. A record of the search was subsequently sent to the public prosecutor's office but was never validated by a member of that office. Applicant alleged the search constituted interference with her right to respect for her home and private life. The ECHR ruled unanimously that, as the Italian Code of Criminal Procedure requires public prosecutor offices to check whether police act lawfully by validating their records of searches within 48 hours of transmission, this failure to follow the statutory procedures violated Article 8 (right to respect for private life) of the *Convention*. In addition, since there is no effective remedy available in Italian law to seek redress for this situation, the ECHR also ruled unanimously that this is a violation of Article 13 (right to an effective remedy).[76]

The Spanish Constitution and Rights

After the 1975 death of Francisco Franco, a seven-person panel (*padres de la Constitucion*) was selected from members of the Spanish Parliament to draft a constitution and then submit it to Parliament for approval. Once approved by

Parliament, and subsequently by the Spanish people, the Spanish Constitution went into effect on 29 December 1978. The Preamble of the Spanish Constitution of 1978 guarantees, among other things, the rule of law, the exercise of human rights, and an advanced democratic society.

Part I of the Constitution (chapters 1-5) describes the fundamental rights and duties of individuals in Spain. Among the rights included in chapters 1 and 2 (Division 1) are equality before the law,[77] freedom of religion,[78] a right to family privacy,[79] no unreasonable entry or search of the home,[80] a right to travel,[81] the right to academic freedom,[82] a right to peaceful unarmed assembly,[83] the right of association,[84] criminal due process rights,[85] and a guarantee of fundamental rights for prisoners (including the right to paid work and appropriate social security benefits).[86] Citizens may assert and have these rights protected by the ordinary courts and, when appropriate, individuals may also lodge an appeal for protection of these rights to the Constitutional Court.[87]

Chapter 3 of this part of the Constitution includes economic and social rights, such as the guarantee of a social security system (including unemployment assistance),[88] the right to health protection (including necessary benefits and services),[89] the right to enjoy decent and adequate housing,[90] and a right to sufficient income for senior citizens.[91] Although the Constitution requires these rights be respected, recognized, and protected by legislators, judges, and public authorities, citizens may only assert and have these rights protected by the ordinary courts "in accordance with the legal provisions implementing them."[92]

Like France, Germany, and Italy, the Spanish legal system is based on a civil code. The underlying theory behind this system is that, by enacting a comprehensive body of laws, lawyers and judges can logically settle disputes by simply discovering the applicable sections of the Code and applying them, without resorting to personal preferences or biases.

The Supreme Court of Spain (*Tribunal Supremo*) is the nation's general court of last resort, possessing jurisdiction over the entire judicial system except those issues relating to the Constitution. The Supreme Court hears appeals from the National Court, as well as from the various regional courts, and is the trial court for cases against members of parliament, including ministers of government and the prime minister. The Spanish judiciary is divided into hierarchical systems of a horizontal nature (civil, criminal, administrative, and social) as well as of a vertical nature (Supreme Court, autonomous communities, provinces, and districts).

The National Court (*Audiencia Nacional*) also possesses jurisdiction over the entire territory of Spain, hearing criminal cases of a national nature, as well as social and administrative jurisdiction cases involving the central government and bureaucracy, or more than one autonomous community. The High Courts of Justice (*Tribunal Superior*) are the highest courts for each of the autonomous communities, while each province has a Provincial Court (*Audiencia Provincial*) which stands as its highest court.

The Constitutional Court of Spain (*Tribunal Constitucional de Espana*) has "jurisdiction over the whole Spanish territory"[93] and possesses the power to determine the constitutional validity of national or regional "acts and statutes having the force of an act."[94] The Constitutional Court can review requests from individuals (for protection of rights and freedoms),[95] national or regional governmental officials,[96] or judicial bodies.[97] Although the Spanish Supreme Court is the court of last resort in all other areas of law, judgments by the Constitutional Court have the force of law once they are published and may not be appealed.[98]

Although Spain has not had as many recent cases before the ECHR as France, Italy, or Germany, there have been a number of important complaints decided by the court involving Spain in the past few years. These include *Pescador v. Spain*,[99] *Puig Panella v. Spain*,[100] *Da Costa v. Spain*,[101] and *Iglesias Gil and A.U.I. v. Spain*.[102] Sixto Jose Pescador Valero, a Spanish national, worked for over a decade in the administrative division of a Spanish university before being removed from his position as head of the administrative staff. He then sought judicial review of the decision in the High Court of Justice. After learning that the presiding judge of the section his case was assigned to was a visiting professor at the same university, Pescador sought an order to have the judge stand down. But his application was dismissed on the grounds Pescador should have been aware of the judge's professional connections and filed his application earlier. Subsequently, the High Court of Justice, presided over by the same judge, found Pescador's removal lawful and the Constitutional Court dismissed the appeal. Although the ECHR found no evidence to suggest the presiding judge was guilty of prejudice, the court considered the case in light of the obligation imposed on judges by the Institutional Law on the Judiciary to stand down whenever they are directly or indirectly connected to litigation. Since Spanish law required the presiding judge to not take part in the case, he should have stood down. In addition, since there was no evidence Pescador had any knowledge of the presiding judge's connections with the university prior to the filing of the case, this situation could legitimately cause the apprehension of impartiality on the part of the applicant, As such, the court unanimously ruled authorities violated Article 6.1 (right to a fair trial).[103]

Jordi Puig Panella, a Spanish national, was arrested and taken into custody on suspicion of having taken part in an attack on a local military headquarters.

The military court eventually convicted him merely on the basis of documents obtained during the investigation stage. Despite the fact that these documents were never produced or submitted for adversarial argument at trial, he was sentenced to prison. After his release, the Constitutional Court allowed his appeal and set aside the military court's decision on the grounds it had infringed on the principle of presumption of innocence. Panella then sought compensation from the Ministry of Justice for the 1,663 days he had spent incarcerated, but the Minister rejected the claim because Panella had not been acquitted or had the charges discontinued. Panella's application for judicial review by the Spanish courts was later dismissed. On review, the ECHR ruled that, although Section 294(1) of the Judicature Act requires either acquittal or that the charges be dropped as a basis for compensation, the Minister's decision to reject the claim for compensation established lingering doubts on Panella's innocence. In addition, the court ruled that the Constitutional Court's assertion that Section 294 (compensation for pretrial detention) was applicable here, rather than applying the broader Section 292 (judicial error or miscarriage of justice), was excessively harsh since Panella had never complained about his pretrial detention. Because these actions by Spanish authorities cast doubts on Panella's innocence (despite the initial judgment of the Constitutional Court to set aside the military court's decision), the ECHR ruled unanimously that this was a violation of Article 6.2 (presumption of innocence).[104]

Carlos Dacosta Silva, a Spanish national, was a member of the Civil Guard when, after hearing of a seriously ill relative and notifying his duty officer, he returned home for a week. His immediate supervisor, considering Dacosta absent without leave, subsequently put him on house arrest for six days. After all of Dacosta's appeals were dismissed, the ECHR chose to review the complaint even though Spain's reservation to Articles 5 and 6 of the *Convention* meant the articles were not to be applied to their armed forces disciplinary rules. Despite this fact, the court ruled the reservation does not apply to the disciplinary rules of the Civil Guard. As a result, the court ruled unanimously that Spanish authorities had deprived Dacosta of his liberty, in violation of Article 5.1 (right to liberty and security).[105]

Maria Iglesias and A.U.I., her son, are Spanish nationals. Although Maria was awarded custody of the child after their divorce, the father (A.U.A.) took advantage of his access to A.U.I. and abducted him to the United States. When Maria lodged criminal complaints against A.U.A. and those of his family members she alleged collaborated in the abduction, all of her requests to the investigating judge were refused, including an application for an international search and seizure warrant. The judge based his rulings on the grounds a parent having joint custody could not be prosecuted for abducting their child. The judge subsequently discontinued the proceedings against A.U.A. because he could not be questioned and therefore charged under the Code of Criminal Procedure. After Maria's appeals were dismissed, she was eventually granted full parental custody of the child and, when A.U. A. returned to Spain with A.U.I. for a visit, Maria took custody of her son with the aid of the police. In reviewing the complaint, the ECHR stated that, as parents have a right to have measures taken to reunite them with their child, national authorities have an obligation to take such action. Since this obligation must be interpreted in respect to the Hague Convention (25 October 1980) on the Civil Aspects of International Child Abduction, to which both Spain and the United States are contracting parties, the issue is whether national parties took all of the steps necessary in this matter. Although the court recognized a number of steps were taken by the Spanish courts, the Hague Convention required Spain to take any and all appropriate measures to secure the return of the child to his mother. Since none of these measures required by the Hague Convention had been taken, the Spanish authorities breached the applicants' Article 8 right to respect for family life.[106]

---

[1] Stein, Peter. ROMAN LAW IN EUROPEAN HISTORY (Cambridge University Press, 1999) p. 3.

[2] Stein, *supra* n.1, p.13.

[3] Stein, *supra* n.1, p.14.

[4] Stein, *supra* n.1, p.28.

[5] Stein, *supra* n.1, p.33.

[6] Calvi, James & Coleman, Susan. AMERICAN LAW AND LEGAL SYSTEMS, 6th Edition (Pearson PrenticeHall, 2008) p.22.

[7] Tarr, G. Alan. JUDICIAL PROCESS AND JUDICIAL POLICYMAKING, 3rd Edition (Thomson Wadsworth, 2003) p. 7.

[8] Stein, *supra* n.1, p.52.

[9] Stein, *supra* n.1, p.64-66.

[10] Stein, *supra* n.1, p.75.

[11] Stein, *supra* n.1, p.104.

[12] Banks, Christopher & O'Brien, David. COURTS AND JUDICIAL POLICYMAKING (Pearson PrenticeHall, 2008) p.5.

[13] Calvi & Coleman, *supra* n. 6, p.23.

[14] Murphy, Walter & Pritchett, C. Herman. COURTS, JUDGES, AND POLITICS, 4th Edition. (McGraw-Hill, 1986) p.10.

[15] Shapiro, Martin. COURTS: A COMPARATIVE AND POLITICAL ANALYSIS. (U. of Chicago Press, 1981) p.135-37.

[16] Shapiro, *supra* n.15, p.150-51.

[17] Calvi & Coleman, *supra* n.6, p.24.

[18] Article 1

[19] Article 2

[20] Hauss, Charles. COMPARATIVE POLITICS, 5th Ed. (Thomson Wadsworth, 2006) p.129.

[21] Article 34

[22] Kesselman, Mark, Krieger, Joel, & Joseph, William. INTRODUCTION TO COMPARATIVE POLITICS, 4th Ed. (Houghton Mifflin Co., 2007) p.126.

[23] Decision n 71-44DC du 16 juillet 1971.

[24] Kesselman, *supra* n.22, p.126.

[25] Article 61: "To the same end, Acts of Parliament may be referred to the Constitutional Council, before their promulgation, by the President of the Republic, the Prime Minister, the President of the National Assembly, the President of the Senate, or sixty deputies or sixty senators. In the cases provided for in the two preceding paragraphs, the Constitutional Council must rule within one month. However, at the request of the Government, if the matter is urgent, this period shall be reduced to eight days."

[26] Kesselman, *supra* n.22, p.126.

[27] ECHR (9375/02, No.101, 2007)

[28] ECHR (70204/01, No.98, 2007)

[29] ECHR (39922/03, No.87, 2006)

[30] ECHR (1914/02, No.98, 2007)

[31] ECHR Press Release issued by the Registrar (665, 9.10.2007)

[32] ECHR Press Release issued by the Registrar (406, 12.6.2007)

[33] ECHR Press Release issued by the Registrar (318, 1.6.2006)

[34] ECHR Press Release issued by the Registrar (390, 7.6.2007)

[35] Kesselman, *supra* n.22, p.171.

[36] Article 1

[37] Article 2

[38] Article 3

[39] Articles 4, 5, 8, and 9

[40] Article 10

[41] Article 13

[42] Article 16a

[43] Kesselman, *supra* n.22, p.177.

[44] Freckmann, Anke & Wegerich, Thomas. THE GERMAN LEGAL SYSTEM. (Sweet & Maxwell, 1999) p.98. "The *Bundesverfassungsgericht* consists of two senates each of them being composed of eight professional judges....These judges are elected by the *Bundestag* and the *Bundesrat*. The powers of each senate hearing a case are specified in (section) 14 BVerfGG. Thereby, the 1st senate is primarily competent for legal disputes concerning basic constitutional rights and the 2nd senate for all legal disputes referring to the law of the constitutional organs."

[45] Jackson, Vicki & Tushnet, Mark. COMPARATIVE CONSTITUTIONAL LAW. (Foundation Press, 1999) p.521.

[46] ECHR (74613/01, No.99, 2007)

[47] ECHR (54810/00, No.88, 2006)

[48] ECHR (77909/01, 2005)

[49] ECHR (61603/00, 2005)

[50] ECHR Press Release issued by the Registrar (503, 12.7.2007)

[51] ECHR Press Release issued by the Registrar (421, 11.7.2006)

[52] ECHR Press Release issued by the Registrar (150, 24.3.2005; Revision 699, 15.12.2005)

[53] ECHR Press Release issued by the Registrar (331, 16.6.2005)
[54] Article 3
[55] Article 13
[56] Article 14
[57] Article 15
[58] Article 16
[59] Article 18
[60] Article 19
[61] Article 21
[62] Article 32
[63] Article 37
[64] Article 38
[65] Shapiro, *supra* n.15, p.144-47.
[66] Article 134
[67] Article 136
[68] Article 137
[69] ECHR (30278/04, No.99, 2007)
[70] ECHR (10075/02, No.2, 2005)
[71] ECHR (39748/98, 2004)
[72] ECHR (60033/00, 2005)
[73] ECHR Press Release issued by the Registrar (515, 17.7.2007)
[74] ECHR Press Release issued by the Registrar (065, 10.02.2005)
[75] ECHR Press Release issued by the Registrar (077, 17.02.2004)
[76] ECHR Press Release issued by the Registrar (060, 8.2.2005)
[77] Section 14
[78] Section 16
[79] Section 18
[80] Section 18
[81] Section 19
[82] Section 20
[83] Section 21
[84] Section 22
[85] Section 24
[86] Section 25
[87] Chapter 4, Section 53
[88] Section 41
[89] Section 43
[90] Section 47
[91] Section 50
[92] Chapter 4, Section 53
[93] Part IX, Section 161(1)
[94] Section 161(2)
[95] Section 161(3) "Individual appeals for protection (*recursos de amparo*) against violation of the rights and freedoms contained in section 53(2) of the Constitution, in the circumstances and manner to be laid down by law."

[96] Section 162(2)
[97] Section 163
[98] Section 164
[99] ECHR (62435/00, 2003)
[100] ECHR (1483/02, 2006)
[101] ECHR (69966/01, 2006)
[102] ECHR (56673/00, 2003)
[103] ECHR Press Release issued by the Registrar (320, 17.6.2003)
[104] ECHR Press Release issued by the Registrar (236, 25.4.2006)
[105] ECHR Press Release issued by the Registrar (658, 2.11.2006)
[106] ECHR Press Release issued by the Registrar (229, 29.4.2003)

French Constitution of 4 October 1958

(Selected Provisions)

PREAMBLE

The French people solemnly proclaim their attachment to the Rights of Man and the principles of national sovereignty as defined by the Declaration of 1789, confirmed and complemented by the Preamble to the Constitution of 1946, and to the rights and duties as defined in the Charter for the Environment of 2004.

By virtue of these principles and that of the self-determination of peoples, the Republic offers to the overseas territories that express the will to adhere to them new institutions founded on the common ideal of liberty, equality and fraternity and conceived with a view to their democratic development.

Article 1

France shall be an indivisible, secular, democratic and social Republic. It shall ensure the equality of all citizens before the law, without distinction of origin, race or religion. It shall respect all beliefs. It shall be organized on a decentralized basis.

TITLE I - On sovereignty

Article 2

The language of the Republic shall be French.

The national emblem shall be the blue, white and red tricolor flag.

The national anthem shall be La Marseillaise.

The motto of the Republic shall be « Liberty, Equality, Fraternity ».

Its principle shall be government of the people, by the people and for the people.

Article 3

National sovereignty shall belong to the people, who shall exercise it through their representatives and by means of referendum.

No section of the people nor any individual may arrogate to itself, or to himself, the exercise thereof.

Suffrage may be direct or indirect as provided by the Constitution. It shall always be universal, equal and secret.

All French citizens of either sex who have reached their majority and are in possession of their civil and political rights may vote as provided by statute.

Article 4

Political parties and groups shall contribute to the exercise of suffrage. They shall be formed and carry on their activities freely. They must respect the principles of national sovereignty and democracy.

TITLE II - The President of the Republic

TITLE III - The Government

TITLE IV - Parliament

TITLE V - On relations between Parliament and the Government

Article 34

Statutes shall be passed by Parliament.

Statutes shall determine the rules concerning:

• civic rights and the fundamental guarantees granted to citizens for the exercise of their public liberties; the obligations imposed for the purposes of national defense upon citizens in respect of their persons and their property;

• nationality, the status and legal capacity of persons, matrimonial regimes, inheritance and gifts;

• the determination of serious crimes and other major offences and the penalties they carry; criminal procedure; amnesty; the setting up of new categories of courts and the status of members of the Judiciary;

• the base, rates and methods of collection of taxes of all types; the issue of currency.

Statutes shall likewise determine the rules concerning:

• the electoral systems of parliamentary assemblies and local assemblies;

• the creation of categories of public establishments;

• the fundamental guarantees granted to civil and military personnel employed by the State;

• the nationalization of enterprises and transfers of ownership in enterprises from the public to the private sector.

Statutes shall determine the fundamental principles of:

• the general organization of national defence;

• the self-government of territorial units, their powers and their resources;

• the preservation of the environment;

• education;

• the regime governing ownership, rights in rem and civil and commercial obligations;

• labor law, trade-union law and social security.

Finance Acts shall determine the resources and obligations of the State in the manner and with the reservations specified in an institutional Act.

Social security finance Acts shall determine the general conditions for the financial balance of social security and, in the light of their revenue forecasts, shall determine expenditure targets in the manner and with the reservations specified in an institutional Act.

Program Acts shall determine the objectives of the economic and social action of the State.

The provisions of this article may be enlarged upon and complemented by an institutional Act.

Article 41

Should it be found in the course of the legislative process that a Member's bill or amendment is not a matter for statute or is contrary to a delegation granted by virtue of article 38, the Government may object that it is inadmissible.

In the event of disagreement between the Government and the President of the assembly concerned, the Constitutional Council, at the request of one or the other, shall rule within eight days.

TITLE VI - On treaties and international agreements

TITLE VII - The Constitutional Council

TITLE VIII - On judicial authority

Article 66

No one shall be arbitrarily detained.

The judicial authority, guardian of individual liberty, shall ensure the observance of this principle as provided by statute.

Article 66-1

No one shall be sentenced to death.

TITLE IX - The High Court

TITLE X - On the criminal liability of members of the government

TITLE XI - The Economic and Social Council

Article 69

The Economic and Social Council, on a referral from the Government, shall give its opinion on such Government Bills, draft Ordinances, draft Decrees, and Private Members' Bills as have been submitted to it.

A member of the Economic and Social Council may be designated by the Council to present, to the parliamentary assemblies, the opinion of the Council on such bills or drafts as have been submitted to it.

Article 70

The Economic and Social Council may likewise be consulted by the Government on any economic or social issue. Any plan or program bill of an economic or social character shall be submitted to it for its opinion.

TITLE XII - On territorial units

TITLE XIII - Transitional provisions relating to New Caledonia

TITLE XIV - On association agreements

TITLE XV - On the European Communities and the European Union

TITLE XV - On the European Union

TITLE XVI - On the amendment of the Constitution

TITLE XVII - *(Repealed)*

CHARTER FOR THE ENVIRONMENT

The French People

Considering that

Natural resources and equilibriums have conditioned the emergence of mankind;

The future and very existence of mankind are inextricably linked with its natural environment;

The environment is the common heritage of all mankind;

Mankind exerts ever-increasing influence over the conditions for life and its own evolution;

Biological diversity, the fulfillment of the person and the progress of human societies are affected by certain types of consumption or production and by excessive exploitation of natural resources ;

Care must be taken to safeguard the environment along with the other fundamental interests of the Nation;

In order to ensure sustainable development, choices designed to meet the needs of the present generation should not jeopardize the ability of future generations and other peoples to meet their own needs,

Hereby proclaim:

Art 1 - Everyone has the right to live in a balanced environment which shows due respect for health.

Art 2 - Everyone is under a duty to participate in preserving and enhancing the environment.

Art 3 - Everyone shall, in the conditions provided for by law, foresee and avoid the occurrence of any damage which he or she may cause to the environment or, failing that, limit the consequences of such damage.

Art 4 - Everyone shall be required, in the conditions provided for by law, to contribute to the making good of any damage he or she may have caused to the environment.

Art 5 - When the occurrence of any damage, albeit unpredictable in the current state of scientific knowledge, may seriously and irreversibly harm the environment, public authorities shall, with due respect for the principle of precaution and the areas within their jurisdiction, ensure the implementation of procedures for risk assessment and the adoption of temporary measures commensurate with the risk involved in order to preclude the occurrence of such damage.

Art 6 - Public policies shall promote sustainable development. To this end they shall reconcile the protection and enhancement of the environment with economic development and social progress.

Art 7 - Everyone has the right, in the conditions and to the extent provided for by law, to have access to information pertaining to the environment in the possession of public bodies and to participate in the public decision-taking process likely to affect the environment.

Art 8 - Education and training with regard to the environment shall contribute to the exercising of the rights and duties set out in this Charter.

Art 9 - Research and innovation shall contribute to the preservation and development of the environment.

Art 10 - This Charter shall inspire France's actions at both European and international levels.

Basic Law
for the Federal Republic of Germany

(Selected Provisions)

23 May 1949

PREAMBLE

Conscious of their responsibility before God and man, Inspired by the determination to promote world peace as an equal partner in a united Europe, the German people, in the exercise of their constituent power, have adopted this Basic Law. Germans in the Länder of Baden-Württemberg, Bavaria, Berlin, Brandenburg, Bremen, Hamburg, Hesse, Lower Saxony, Mecklenburg- Western Pomerania, North Rhine-Westphalia, Rhineland-Palatinate, Saarland, Saxony, Saxony-Anhalt, Schleswig-Holstein, and Thuringia have achieved the unity and freedom of Germany in free self-determination. This Basic Law thus applies to the entire German people.

I. Basic Rights

Article 1 [Human dignity]

(1) Human dignity shall be inviolable. To respect and protect it shall be the duty of all state authority.

(2) The German people therefore acknowledge inviolable and inalienable human rights as the basis of every community, of peace and of justice in the world.

(3) The following basic rights shall bind the legislature, the executive, and the judiciary as directly applicable law.

Article 2 [Personal freedoms]

(1) Every person shall have the right to free development of his personality insofar as he does not violate the rights of others or offend against the constitutional order or the moral law.

(2) Every person shall have the right to life and physical integrity. Freedom of the person shall be inviolable. These rights may be interfered with only pursuant to a law.

Article 3 [Equality before the law]

(1) All persons shall be equal before the law.

(2) Men and women shall have equal rights. The state shall promote the actual implementation of equal rights for women and men and take steps to eliminate disadvantages that now exist.

(3) No person shall be favored or disfavored because of sex, parentage, race, language, homeland and origin, faith, or religious or political opinions. No person shall be disfavored because of disability.

Article 4 [Freedom of faith, conscience, and creed]

(1) Freedom of faith and of conscience, and freedom to profess a religious or philosophical creed, shall be inviolable.

(2) The undisturbed practice of religion shall be guaranteed.

(3) No person shall be compelled against his conscience to render military service involving the use of arms. Details shall be regulated by a federal law.

Article 5 [Freedom of expression]

(1) Every person shall have the right freely to express and disseminate his opinions in speech, writing, and pictures and to inform himself without hindrance from generally accessible sources. Freedom of the press and freedom of reporting by means of broadcasts and films shall be guaranteed. There shall be no censorship.

(2) These rights shall find their limits in the provisions of general laws, in provisions for the protection of young persons, and in the right to personal honor.

(3) Art and scholarship, research, and teaching shall be free. The freedom of teaching shall not release any person from allegiance to the constitution.

Article 6 [Marriage and the family; children born outside of marriage]

(1) Marriage and the family shall enjoy the special protection of the state.

(2) The care and upbringing of children is the natural right of parents and a duty primarily incumbent upon them. The state shall watch over them in the performance of this duty.

(3) Children may be separated from their families against the will of their parents or guardians only pursuant to a law, and only if the parents or guardians fail in their duties or the children are otherwise in danger of serious neglect.

(4) Every mother shall be entitled to the protection and care of the community.

(5) Children born outside of marriage shall be provided by legislation with the same opportunities for physical and mental development and for their position in society as are enjoyed by those born within marriage.

Article 7 [School education]

(1) The entire school system shall be under the supervision of the state.

(2) Parents and guardians shall have the right to decide whether children shall receive religious instruction.

(3) Religious instruction shall form part of the regular curriculum in state schools, with the exception of non-denominational schools. Without prejudice to the state's right of supervision, religious instruction shall be given in accordance with the tenets of the religious community concerned. Teachers may not be obliged against their will to give religious instruction.

(4) The right to establish private schools shall be guaranteed. Private schools that serve as alternatives to state schools shall require the approval of the State and

shall be subject to the laws of the Länder. Such approval shall be given when private schools are not inferior to the state schools in terms of their educational aims, their facilities, or the professional training of their teaching staff, and when segregation of pupils according to the means of their parents will not be encouraged thereby. Approval shall be withheld if the economic and legal position of the teaching staff is not adequately assured.

(5) A private elementary school shall be approved only if the educational authority finds that it serves a special pedagogical interest or if, on the application of parents or guardians, it is to be established as a denominational or interdenominational school or as a school based on a particular philosophy and no state elementary school of that type exists in the municipality.

(6) Preparatory schools shall remain abolished.

Article 8 [Freedom of assembly]

(1) All Germans shall have the right to assemble peacefully and unarmed without prior notification or permission.

(2) In the case of outdoor assemblies, this right may be restricted by or pursuant to a law.

Article 9 [Freedom of association]

(1) All Germans shall have the right to form corporations and other associations.

(2) Associations whose aims or activities contravene the criminal laws, or that are directed against the constitutional order or the concept of international understanding, shall be prohibited.

(3) The right to form associations to safeguard and improve working and economic conditions shall be guaranteed to every individual and to every occupation or profession. Agreements that restrict or seek to impair this right shall be null and void; measures directed to this end shall be unlawful. Measures taken pursuant to Article 12a, to paragraphs (2) and (3) of Article 35, to paragraph (4) of Article 87a, or to Article 91 may not be directed against industrial disputes engaged in by associations within the meaning of the first sentence of this paragraph in order to safeguard and improve working and economic conditions.

Article 10 [Privacy of correspondence, posts and telecommunications]

(1) The privacy of correspondence, posts and telecommunications shall be inviolable.

(2) Restrictions may be ordered only pursuant to a law. If the restriction serves to protect the free democratic basic order or the existence or security of the Federation or of a Land, the law may provide that the person affected shall not be informed of the restriction and that recourse to the courts shall be replaced by a review of the case by agencies and auxiliary agencies appointed by the legislature.

Article 11 [Freedom of movement]

(1) All Germans shall have the right to move freely throughout the federal territory.

(2) This right may be restricted only by or pursuant to a law, and only in cases in which the absence of adequate means of support would result in a particular burden for the community, or in which such restriction is necessary to avert an imminent danger to the existence or the free democratic basic order of the Federation or of a Land, to combat the danger of an epidemic, to respond to a grave accident or natural disaster, to protect young persons from serious neglect, or to prevent crime.

Article 12 [Occupational freedom; prohibition of forced labor]

(1) All Germans shall have the right freely to choose their occupation or profession, their place of work, and their place of training. The practice of an occupation or profession may be regulated by or pursuant to a law.

(2) No person may be required to perform work of a particular kind except within the framework of a traditional duty of community service that applies generally and equally to all.

(3) Forced labor may be imposed only on persons deprived of their liberty by the judgment of a court.

Article 12 a [Compulsory military or alternative service]

(1) Men who have attained the age of eighteen may be required to serve in the Armed Forces, in the Federal Border Police, or in a civil defense organization.

(2) Any person who, on grounds of conscience, refuses to render military service involving the use of arms may be required to perform alternative service. The duration of alternative service shall not exceed that of military service. Details shall be regulated by a law, which shall not interfere with the freedom to make a decision in accordance with the dictates of conscience, and which shall also provide for the possibility of alternative service not connected with units of the Armed Forces or of the Federal Border Police.

(3) Persons liable to compulsory military service who are not called upon to render service pursuant to paragraph (1) or (2) of this Article may, when a state of defense is in effect, be assigned by or pursuant to a law to employment involving civilian services for defense purposes, including the protection of the civilian population; they may be assigned to public employment only for the purpose of discharging police functions or such other sovereign functions of public administration as can be discharged only by persons employed in the public service. The employment contemplated by the first sentence of this paragraph may include services within the Armed Forces, in the provision of military supplies, or with public administrative authorities; assignments to employment connected with supplying and servicing the civilian

population shall be permissible only to meet their basic requirements or to guarantee their safety.

(4) If, during a state of defense, the need for civilian services in the civilian health system or in stationary military hospitals cannot be met on a voluntary basis, women between the ages of eighteen and fiftyfive may be called upon to render such services by or pursuant to a law. They may under no circumstances be required to bear weapons.

(5) Prior to the existence of a state of defense, assignments under paragraph (3) of this Article may be made only if the requirements of paragraph (1) of Article 80a are met. In preparation for the provision of services under paragraph (3) of this Article that demand special knowledge or skills, participation in training courses may be required by or pursuant to a law. In this case the first sentence of this paragraph shall not apply.

(6) If, during a state of defense, the need for workers in the areas specified in the second sentence of paragraph (3) of this Article cannot be met on a voluntary basis, the right of German citizens to abandon their occupation or place of employment may be restricted by or pursuant to a law in order to meet this need. Prior to the existence of a state of defense, the first sentence of paragraph (5) of this Article shall apply mutatis mutandis.

Article 13 [Inviolability of the home]

(1) The home is inviolable.

(2) Searches may be authorized only by a judge or, when time is of the essence, by other authorities designated by the laws, and may be carried out only in the manner therein prescribed.

(3) If particular facts justify the suspicion that any person has committed an especially serious crime specifically defined by a law, technical means of acoustical surveillance of any home in which the suspect is supposedly staying may be employed pursuant to judicial order for the purpose of prosecuting the offense, provided that alternative methods of investigating the matter would be disproportionately difficult or unproductive. The authorization shall be for a limited time. The order shall be issued by a panel composed of three judges. When time is of the essence, it may also be issued by a single judge.

(4) To avert acute dangers to public safety, especially dangers to life or to the public, technical means of surveillance of the home may be employed only pursuant to judicial order. When time is of the essence, such measures may also be ordered by other authorities designated by a law; a judicial decision shall subsequently be obtained without delay.

(5) If technical means are contemplated solely for the protection of persons officially deployed in a home, the measure may be ordered by an authority designated by a law. The information thereby obtained may be otherwise used only for purposes of criminal prosecution or to avert danger and only if the legality of the measure has been previously determined by a judge; when time is of the essence, a judicial decision shall subsequently be obtained without delay.

(6) The Federal Government shall report to the Bundestag annually as to the employment of technical means pursuant to paragraph (3) and, within the jurisdiction of the Federation, pursuant to paragraph (4) and, insofar as judicial approval is required, pursuant to paragraph (5) of this Article. A panel elected by the Bundestag shall exercise parliamentary control on the basis of this report. A comparable parliamentary control shall be afforded by the Länder.

(7) Interferences and restrictions shall otherwise only be permissible to avert a danger to the public or to the life of an individual, or, pursuant to a law, to confront an acute danger to public safety and order, in particular to relieve a housing shortage, to combat the danger of an epidemic, or to protect young persons at risk.

Article 14 [Property, inheritance, expropriation]

(1) Property and the right of inheritance shall be guaranteed. Their content and limits shall be defined by the laws.

(2) Property entails obligations. Its use shall also serve the public good.

(3) Expropriation shall only be permissible for the public good. It may only be ordered by or pursuant to a law that determines the nature and extent of compensation. Such compensation shall be determined by establishing an equitable balance between the public interest and the interests of those affected. In case of dispute respecting the amount of compensation, recourse may be had to the ordinary courts.

Article 15 [Socialization]

Land, natural resources, and means of production may for the purpose of socialization be transferred to public ownership or other forms of public enterprise by a law that determines the nature and extent of compensation. With respect to such compensation the third and fourth sentences of paragraph (3) of Article 14 shall apply mutatis mutandis.

Article 16 [Citizenship; extradition]

(1) No German may be deprived of his citizenship. Citizenship may be lost only pursuant to a law, and against the will of the person affected only if he does not become stateless as a result.

(2) No German may be extradited to a foreign country. A different regulation to cover extradition to a Member State of the European Union or to an international

court of law may be laid down by law, provided that constitutional principles are observed.

Article 16 a [Right of asylum]

(1) Persons persecuted on political grounds shall have the right of asylum.

(2) Paragraph (1) of this Article may not be invoked by a person who enters the federal territory from a member state of the European Communities or from another third state in which application of the Convention Relating to the Status of Refugees and of the Convention for the Protection of Human Rights and Fundamental Freedoms is assured. The states outside the European Communities to which the criteria of the first sentence of this paragraph apply shall be specified by a law requiring the consent of the Bundesrat.

In the cases specified in the first sentence of this paragraph, measures to terminate an applicant's stay may be implemented without regard to any legal challenge that may have been instituted against them.

(3) By a law requiring the consent of the Bundesrat, states may be specified in which, on the basis of their laws, enforcement practices, and general political conditions, it can be safely concluded that neither political persecution nor inhuman or degrading punishment or treatment exists. It shall be presumed that a foreigner from such a state is not persecuted, unless he presents evidence justifying the conclusion that, contrary to this presumption, he is persecuted on political grounds.

(4) In the cases specified by paragraph (3) of this Article and in other cases that are plainly unfounded or considered to be plainly unfounded, the implementation of measures to terminate an applicant's stay may be suspended by a court only if serious doubts exist as to their legality; the scope of review may be limited, and tardy objections may be disregarded. Details shall be determined by a law.

(5) Paragraphs (1) through (4) of this Article shall not preclude the conclusion of international agreements of member states of the European Communities with each other or with those third states which, with due regard for the obligations arising from the Convention Relating to the Status of Refugees and the Convention for the Protection of Human Rights and Fundamental Freedoms, whose enforcement must be assured in the contracting states, adopt rules conferring jurisdiction to decide on applications for asylum, including the reciprocal recognition of asylum decisions.

Article 17 [Right of petition]

Every person shall have the right individually or jointly with others to address written requests or complaints to competent authorities and to the legislature.

Article 17 a [Restriction of certain basic rights by laws respecting defense and

alternative service]

(1) Laws respecting military and alternative service may provide that the basic right of members of the Armed Forces and of alternative service freely to express and disseminate their opinions in speech, writing, and pictures (first clause of paragraph (1) of Article 5), the basic right of assembly (Article 8), and the right of petition (Article 17) insofar as it permits the submission of requests or complaints jointly with others, be restricted during their period of military or alternative service.

(2) Laws respecting defense, including protection of the civilian population, may provide for restriction of the basic rights of freedom of movement (Article 11) and inviolability of the home (Article 13).

Article 18 [Forfeiture of basic rights]

Whoever abuses the freedom of expression, in particular the freedom of the press (paragraph (1) of Article 5), the freedom of teaching (paragraph (3) of Article 5), the freedom of assembly (Article 8), the freedom of association (Article 9), the privacy of correspondence, posts and telecommunications (Article 10), the rights of property (Article 14), or the right of asylum (Article 16a) in order to combat the free democratic basic order shall forfeit these basic rights. This forfeiture and its extent shall be declared by the Federal Constitutional Court.

Article 19 [Restriction of basic rights]

(1) Insofar as, under this Basic Law, a basic right may be restricted by or pursuant to a law, such law must apply generally and not merely to a single case. In addition, the law must specify the basic right affected and the Article in which it appears.

(2) In no case may the essence of a basic right be affected.

(3) The basic rights shall also apply to domestic artificial persons to the extent that the nature of such rights permits.

(4) Should any person's rights be violated by public authority, he may have recourse to the courts. If no other jurisdiction has been established, recourse shall be to the ordinary courts. The second sentence of paragraph (2) of Article 10 shall not be affected by this paragraph.

From *Basic Law for the Federal Republic of Germany*, December 2000.
Reprinted by permission of the Consulate General of the Federal Republic of Germany.

THE CONSTITUTION OF ITALY

(Selected Provisions)

Fundamental Principles

Article 1   Form of State

(1) Italy is a democratic republic based on labor.

(2) The sovereignty belongs to the people who exercise it in the forms and limits of the constitution.

Article 2   Human Rights

The republic recognizes and guarantees the inviolable human rights, be it as an individual or in social groups expressing their personality, and it ensures the performance of the unalterable duty to political, economic, and social solidarity.

Article 3   Equality

(1) All citizens have equal social status and are equal before the law, without regard to their sex, race, language, religion, political opinions, and personal or social conditions.

(2) It is the duty of the republic to remove all economic and social obstacles that, by limiting the freedom and equality of citizens, prevent full individual development and the participation of all workers in the political, economic, and social organization of the country.

Article 4   Work

(1) The republic recognizes the right of all citizens to work and promotes conditions to fulfill this right.

(2) According to capability and choice, every citizen has the duty to undertake an activity or a function that will contribute to the material and moral progress of society.

Article 5   Local Autonomy

The republic, one and indivisible, recognizes and promotes local autonomy; it fully applies administrative decentralization of state services and adopts principles and methods of legislation meeting the requirements of autonomy and decentralization.

Article 6   Linguistic Minorities
The republic protects linguistic minorities by special laws.

Article 7   Relation between State and Church
(1) State and catholic church are, each within their own reign, independent and sovereign.
(2) Their relationship is regulated by the lateran pacts. Amendments to these pacts which are accepted by both parties do not require the procedure of constitutional amendments.

Article 8   Religion
(1) Religious denominations are equally free before the law.
(2) Denominations other than catholicism have the right to organize themselves according to their own by-laws, provided they do not conflict with the Italian legal system.
(3) Their relationship with the state is regulated by law, based on agreements with their representatives.

Article 9   Research and Culture
(1) The republic promotes cultural development and scientific and technical research.
(2) It safeguards natural beauty and the historical and artistic heritage of the nation.

Article 10   International Law
(1) The legal system of Italy conforms to the generally recognized principles of international law.
(2) Legal regulation of the status of foreigners conforms to international rules and treaties.
(3) Foreigners who are, in their own country, denied the actual exercise of those democratic freedoms guaranteed by the Italian constitution, are entitled to the right to asylum under those conditions provided by law.
(4) Foreigners may not be extradited for political offences.

Article 11   Repudiation of War
Italy repudiates war as an instrument offending the liberty of the peoples and as a means for settling international disputes; it agrees to limitations of sovereignty where they are necessary to allow for a legal system of peace and justice between

nations, provided the principle of reciprocity is guaranteed; it promotes and encourages international organizations furthering such ends.

Article 12   Flag

The flag of the republic is the Italian tricolor: green, white, and red, in three vertical bands of equal dimensions.

Part I Rights and Duties of Citizens

Title I Civil Rights

Article 13   Personal Liberty

(1) Personal liberty is inviolable.

(2) No one may be detained, inspected, or searched nor otherwise restricted in personal liberty except by order of the judiciary stating a reason and only in such cases and in such manner as provided by law.

(3) As an exception, under the conditions of necessity and urgency strictly defined by law, the police may take provisional measures that must be reported within 48 hours to the judiciary and, if they are not ratified within another 48 hours, are considered revoked and remain without effect.

(4) Acts of physical and moral violence against persons subjected to restrictions of personal liberty are to be punished.

(5) The law establishes the maximum duration of preventive detention.

Article 14   Personal Domicile

(1) Personal domicile is inviolable.

(2) No one's domicile may be inspected, searched, or seized save in cases and in the manner laid down by law conforming to the guarantee of personal liberty.

(3) Verifications and inspections for public health and safety, or for economic and fiscal purposes are defined by law.

Article 15   Freedom of Correspondence

(1) Liberty and secrecy of correspondence and other forms of communication are inviolable.

(2) Limitations may only be imposed by judicial decision stating the reasons and in accordance with guarantees defined by law.

Article 16   Freedom of Movement

(1) Every citizen has the right to reside and travel freely in any part of the national

territory except for limitations provided by general laws protecting health or security. No restriction may be imposed for political reasons.

(2) Every citizen is free to leave the territory of the republic and return to it except for obligations defined by law.

Article 17   Right of Assembly

(1) All citizens have the right to assemble peaceably and unarmed.

(2) For meetings, including those held in places to which the general public has access, no previous notice is required.

(3) For meetings held in public places previous notice must be given to the authorities, who may prohibit them only on the ground of proven risks to security or public safety.

Article 18   Freedom of Association

(1) Citizens have the right freely and without authorization to form associations for those aims not forbidden by criminal law.

(2) Secret associations and associations pursuing political aims by military organization, even if only indirectly, are forbidden.

Article 19   Freedom of Religion

Everyone is entitled to freely profess religious beliefs in any form, individually or with others, to promote them, and to celebrate rites in public or in private, provided they are not offensive to public morality.

Article 20   Religious Associations

For associations or institutions, their religious character or religious or confessional aims do not justify special limitations or fiscal burdens regarding their establishment, legal capacity, or activities.

Article 21   Freedom of Communication

(1) Everyone has the right to freely express thoughts in speech, writing, and by other communication.

(2) The press may not be controlled by authorization or submitted to censorship.

(3) Seizure is permitted only by judicial order stating the reason and only for offenses expressly determined by the press law or for violation of the obligation to identify the persons responsible for such offences.

(4) In cases of absolute urgency where immediate judicial intervention is impossible, periodicals may be seized by the judicial police, who must immediately and in no case later than 24 hours report the matter to the judiciary.

If the measure is not validated by the judiciary within another 24 hours, it is considered revoked and has no effect.

(5) The law may, by general provision, order the disclosure of financial sources of periodical publications.

(6) Publications, performances, and other exhibits offensive to public morality are prohibited. Measures of prevention and repression against violations are provided by law.

Article 22   Citizenship and Name
Nobody may be deprived of legal capacity, citizenship, or name for political reasons.

Article 23   Personal Services
Nobody may be forced to perform personal service or payment without legal provision.

Article 24   Right to be Heard in Court
(1) Everyone may bring cases before a court of law in order to protect their rights under civil and administrative law.

(2) Defense is an inviolable right at every stage and instance of legal proceedings.

(3) The poor are entitled by law to proper means for action or defense in all courts.

(4) The law defines the conditions and forms for reparation in the case of judicial errors.

Article 25   Defendant's Rights
(1) No case may be removed from a court, but must be heard as provided by law.

(2) No punishment is allowed except provided by a law already in force when the offence has been committed.

(3) Security measures against persons are only allowed as provided by law.

Article 26   Extradition
(1) A citizen may be extradited only as expressly provided by international conventions.

(2) In any case, extradition may not be permitted for political offences.

Article 27   Rights of the Accused
(1) Criminal responsibility is personal.

(2) The defendant may not be considered guilty until sentenced.

(3) Punishments may not contradict humanity and must aim at re-educating the convicted.

(4) Death penalty is prohibited except by military law in time of war.

Article 28   Responsibility of Public Officials

State officials and employees of other public bodies are directly responsible under criminal, civil, and administrative law for acts committed in violation of rights. Civil liability extends to the state and public bodies.

Title II Ethical and Social Relations

Article 29   Marriage

(1) The family is recognized by the republic as a natural association founded on marriage.

(2) Marriage entails moral and legal equality of the spouses within legally defined limits to protect the unity of the family.

Article 30   Parental Duties and Rights

(1) Parents have the duty and right to support, instruct, and educate their children, including those born out of wedlock.

(2) The law provides for the fulfillment of those duties should the parents prove incapable.

(3) Full legal and social protection for children born out of wedlock is guaranteed by law, consistent with the rights of other family members.

(4) Rules and limits to determine paternity are set by law.

Article 31   Family

(1) The republic furthers family formation and the fulfillment of related tasks by means of economic and other provisions with special regard to large families.

(2) The republic protects maternity, infancy, and youth; it supports and encourages institutions needed for this purpose.

Article 32   Health

(1) The republic protects individual health as a basic right and in the public interest; it provides free medical care to the poor.

(2) Nobody may be forcefully submitted to medical treatment except as regulated by law. That law may in no case violate the limits imposed by the respect for the human being.

Article 33   Freedom of Arts, Science and Teaching

(1) The arts and sciences as well as their teaching are free.

(2) The republic adopts general norms for education and establishes public schools of all kinds and grades

(3) Public and private bodies have the right to establish schools and educational institutes without financial obligations to the state.

(4) The law defining rights and obligations of those private schools requesting recognition has to guarantee full liberty to them and equal treatment with pupils of public schools.

(5) Exams are defined for admission to various types and grades of schools, as final course exams, and for professional qualification.

(6) Institutions of higher learning, universities, and academies have the autonomy to establish by-laws within the limits of state law.

Article 34   Education

(1) Schools are open to everyone.

(2) Primary education, given for at least eight years, is compulsory and free of tuition.

(3) Pupils of ability and merit, even if lacking financial resources, have the right to attain the highest grades of studies.

(4) The republic furthers the realization of this right by scholarships, allowances to families, and other provisions, to be assigned through competitive examinations.

Title III Economic Relations

Article 35   Labor

(1) The republic protects labor in all its forms.

(2) It provides for the training and professional enhancement of workers.

(3) It promotes and encourages international treaties and institutions aiming to assert and regulate labor rights.

(4) It recognizes the freedom to emigrate, except for legal limitations for the common good, and protects Italian labor abroad.

Article 36   Wages

(1) Workers are entitled to remuneration commensurate with the quantity and quality of their work, and in any case sufficient to ensure to them and their families a free and honorable existence.

(2) The law establishes limits to the length of the working day.

(3) Workers are entitled to a weekly day of rest and to annual paid holidays; they cannot relinquish this right.

Article 37   Equality of Women at Work
(1) Working women are entitled to equal rights and, for comparable jobs, equal pay as men. Working conditions have to be such as to allow women to fulfill their essential family duties and ensure an adequate protection of mothers and children.
(2) The law defines a minimal age for paid labor.
(3) The republic establishes special measures protecting juvenile labor and guarantees equal pay for comparable work.

Article 38   Welfare
(1) All citizens unable to work and lacking the resources necessary for their existence are entitled to private and social assistance.
(2) Workers are entitled to adequate insurance for their needs in case of accident, illness, disability, old age, and involuntary unemployment.
(3) Disabled and handicapped persons are entitled to education and vocational training.
(4) These responsibilities are entrusted to public bodies and institutions established or supplemented by the state.
(5) Private welfare work is free.

Article 39   Trade Unions
(1) The organization of trade unions is free.
(2) No obligation may be imposed on trade unions except the duty to register at local or central offices as provided by law.
(3) Trade unions are only registered on condition that their by-laws lead to internal organization of democratic character.
(4) Registered trade unions are legal persons. Being represented in proportion to their registered members, they may jointly enter into collective labor contracts which are mandatory for all who belong to the respective industry of these contracts.

Article 40   Right to Strike
The right to strike is exercised according to the law.

Article 41   Freedom of Enterprise
(1) Private economic enterprise is free.
(2) It may not be carried out against the common good or in a way that may harm

public security, liberty, or human dignity.

(3) The law determines appropriate planning and controls so that public and private economic activities may be directed and coordinated towards social ends.

Article 42   Property

(1) Property is public or private. Economic goods may belong to the state, to public bodies, or to private persons.

(2) Private ownership is recognized and guaranteed by laws determining the manner of acquisition and enjoyment and its limits, in order to ensure its social function and to make it accessible to all.

(3) Private property, in cases determined by law and with compensation, may be expropriated for reasons of common interest.

(4) The law establishes the rules of legitimate and testamentary succession and its limits and the state's right to the heritage.

Article 43   Expropriation

To the end of the general good, the law may reserve establishment or transfer, by expropriation with compensation, to the state, public bodies, or workers or consumer communities, specific enterprises or categories of enterprises of primary common interest for essential public services or energy sources, or act as monopolies in the preeminent public interest.

Article 44   Land

(1) For the purpose of ensuring rational utilization of land and establishing equitable social relations, the law imposes obligations on and limitations to private ownership of land, defines its limits depending on the regions and the various agricultural areas, encourages and imposes land cultivation, transformation of large estates, and the reorganization of productive units; it assists small and medium sized farms.

(2) The law favors mountainous areas.

Article 45   Cooperatives and Handicrafts

(1) The republic recognizes the social function of cooperation for mutual benefit free of private speculation. The law promotes and encourages its implementation with suitable provisions and ensures its character and purposes through proper controls.

(2) The law protects and promotes the development of handicrafts.

Article 46　Workers' Participation

In order to achieve the economic and social enhancement of labor and in accordance with the requirements of production, the republic recognizes the right of workers to collaborate, within the forms and limits defined by law, in the management of companies.

Article 47　Savings

(1) The republic encourages and protects savings in all its forms, regulates, coordinates and controls the provision of credit.

(2) It favors access savings for the purchase of homes, for worker-owned farms, and for direct or indirect investment in shares of the country's large productive enterprises.

Title IV Political Rights

Article 48　Voting Rights

(1) All citizens, men or women, who have attained their majority are entitled to vote.

(2) Voting is personal, equal, free, and secret. Its exercise is a civic duty.

(3) The law defines the conditions under which the citizens residing abroad effectively exercise their electoral right. To this end, a constituency of Italians abroad is established for the election of the Chambers, to which a fixed number of seats is assigned by constitutional law in accordance with criteria determined by law.

(4) The right to vote may not be limited except for incapacity, as a consequence of an irrevocable criminal sentence, or in cases of moral unworthiness established by law.

Article 49　Political Parties

All citizens have the right to freely associate in political parties in order to contribute by democratic methods to determine national policy.

Article 50　Petitions

All citizens may address petitions to the Chambers demanding legislative measures or presenting general needs.

Article 51　Public Offices

(1) Citizens of one or the other sex are eligible for public office and for elective positions under equal conditions, according to the rules established by law. To

this end, the republic adopts specific measures in order to promote equal chances for men and women.

(2) The law may, regarding their right to be selected for public positions and elective offices, grant to those Italians who do not belong to the republic the same opportunities as citizens.

(3) Anyone elected to public office is entitled to the time necessary for the fulfillment of the respective duties while keeping his or her job.

Article 52   Military Service

(1) The defense of the fatherland is the sacred duty of every citizen.

(2) Military service is compulsory within the limits and under the terms of the law. The fulfillment of military duties may not prejudice a citizen's position as an employee, nor the exercise of his political rights.

(3) The rules about armed forces must conform to the democratic spirit of the republic.

Article 53   Taxation

(1) Everyone has to contribute to public expenditure in proportion to their capacity.

(2) The tax system has to conform to the principle of progression.

Article 54   Loyalty to the Constitution

(1) All citizens have the duty to be loyal to the republic and to observe the constitution and the laws.

(2) Citizens entrusted with public functions must perform them with discipline and honor, and take an oath of office where required by law.

"The Fundamental Principles." The Articles of the Italian Constitution printed herein are those of the ICL Edition as edited by Professor Carlo Fusaro (and updated to June 2008). Reprinted by permission of Professor Carlo Fusaro, www.servat.unibe.ch/law/icl/it_index.html.

The Spanish Constitution of 1978

(Selected Provisions)

PREAMBLE

The Spanish Nation, desiring to establish justice, liberty and security, and to promote the well-being of all its members, in the exercise of its sovereignty, proclaims its will to:

Guarantee democratic co-existence under the Constitution and the law, in accordance with a fair social and economic order; Consolidate a State of Law which ensures the rule of law as an expression of the popular will; Protect all Spaniards and peoples of Spain in the exercise of human rights, of their cultures and traditions, and of their languages and institutions; Promote the progress of culture and of the economy in order to ensure a worthy quality of life for all; Establish a democratic and advanced society; and Collaborate in the strengthening of peaceful relations and effective cooperation amongst all the peoples of the world. Wherefore, the Cortes pass and the Spanish people ratify the following

PRELIMINARY PART

Article 1

1. Spain is hereby established as a social and democratic State, subject to the rule of law, which advocates as the highest values of its legal order, liberty, justice, equality and political pluralism.

2. National sovereignty is vested in the Spanish people, from whom emanate the powers of the State.

3. The political form of the Spanish State is that of a parliamentary monarchy.

Article 2

The Constitution is based on the indissoluble unity of the Spanish nation, the common and indivisible country of all Spaniards; it recognizes and guarantees the right to autonomy of the nationalities and regions of which it is composed, and the solidarity amongst them all.

Article 3

1. Castilian is the official Spanish language of the State. All Spaniards have the duty to know it and the right to use it.

2. The other Spanish languages shall also be official in the respective Autonomous Communities in accordance with their Statutes.

3. The wealth of the different language modalities of Spain is a cultural heritage which shall be the object of special respect and protection.

Article 4

1. The flag of Spain consists of three horizontal stripes: red, yellow and red, the yellow stripe being double the width of each red stripe.

2. The Statutes may recognize flags and ensigns of the Autonomous Communities. These shall be used together with the flag of Spain on their public buildings and in their official ceremonies.

Article 5

1. The capital of the State is the city of Madrid.

Article 6

Political parties are the expression of political pluralism; they contribute to the formation and expression of the will of the people and are a fundamental instrument for political participation. Their creation and the exercise of their activities are free in so far as they respect the Constitution and the law. Their internal structure and operation must be democratic.

Article 7

Trade unions and employers associations contribute to the defense and promotion of the economic and social interests which they represent. Their creation and the exercise of their activities shall be unrestricted in so far as they respect the Constitution and the law. Their internal structure and operation must be democratic.

Article 8

1. The mission of the Armed Forces, comprising the Army, the Navy and the Air Force, is to guarantee the sovereignty and independence of Spain and to defend its territorial integrity and the constitutional order.

2. The basic structure of military organization shall be regulated by an organic law in accordance with the principles of the Constitution.

Article 9

1. Citizens and public authorities are bound by the Constitution and all other legal provisions.

2. It is incumbent upon the public authorities to promote conditions which ensure that the freedom and equality of individuals and of the groups to which they belong may be real and effective, to remove the obstacles which prevent or hinder their full enjoyment, and to facilitate the participation of all citizens in political, economic, cultural and social life.

3. The Constitution guarantees the principle of legality, the hierarchy of legal provisions, the publicity of legal enactments, the non-retroactivity of punitive measures that are unfavorable to or restrict individual rights, the certainty that the rule of law will prevail, the accountability of the public authorities, and the prohibition against arbitrary action on the part of the latter.

PART I
Article 10
1. The human dignity, the inviolable and inherent rights, the free development of the personality, the respect for the law and for the rights of others are the foundation of political order and social peace.

2. The principles relating to the fundamental rights and liberties recognized by the Constitution shall be interpreted in conformity with the Universal Declaration of Human Rights and the international treaties and agreements thereon ratified by Spain.

CHAPTER ONE

Spaniards and Aliens

Article 11
1. Spanish nationality is acquired, retained and lost in accordance with the provisions of the law.

2. No person of Spanish origin may be deprived of his or her nationality.

3. The State may negotiate dual nationality treaties with Latin- American countries or with those which have had or which have special links with Spain. In these countries, Spaniards may become naturalized without losing their nationality of origin, even if said countries do not recognize a reciprocal right to their own citizens.

Article 12
Spaniards legally come of age at eighteen.

Article 13
1. Aliens shall enjoy the public freedoms guaranteed by the present Title, under the terms to be laid down by treaties and the law.

2. Only Spaniards shall be entitled to the rights recognized in Article 23, except in cases which may be established by treaty or by law concerning the right to vote and the right to be elected in municipal elections, in accordance with the principle of reciprocity.

3. Extradition shall be granted only in compliance with a treaty or with the law, on the basis of the principle of reciprocity. Extradition shall be excluded for political offences; but acts of terrorism shall not be regarded as such.

4. The law shall establish the terms under which citizens from other countries and stateless persons may enjoy the right to asylum in Spain.

CHAPTER TWO

Rights and Liberties

Article 14

Spaniards are equal before the law and may not in any way be discriminated against on account of birth, race, sex, religion, opinion or any other personal or social condition or circumstance.

SECTION 1

Fundamental Rights and Public Liberties

Article 15

Everyone has the right to life and to physical and moral integrity, and may under no circumstances be subjected to torture or to inhuman or degrading punishment or treatment. The death penalty is hereby abolished, except as provided by military criminal law in times of war.

Article 16

1. Freedom of ideology, religion and worship of individuals and communities is guaranteed, with no other restriction on their expression than may be necessary to maintain public order as protected by law.

2. No one may be compelled to make statements regarding his religion, beliefs or ideologies.

3. There shall be no State religion. The public authorities shall take the religious beliefs of Spanish society into account and shall consequently maintain appropriate cooperation with the Catholic Church and the other confessions.

Article 17

1. Every person has a right to freedom and security. No one may be deprived of his or her freedom except in accordance with the provisions of this article and in the cases and in the manner provided by the law.

2. Preventive detention may last no longer than the time strictly required in order to carry out the necessary investigations aimed at establishing the facts; in any case the person arrested must be set free or handed over to the judicial authorities within a maximum period of seventy-two hours.

3. Any person arrested must be informed immediately, and in a manner understandable to him or her, of his or her rights and of the grounds for his or her arrest, and may not be compelled to make a statement. The arrested person shall be guaranteed the assistance of a lawyer during police and judicial proceedings, under the terms established by the law.

4. A *habeas corpus* procedure shall be regulated by law in order to ensure the immediate handing over to the judicial authorities of any person arrested illegally. Likewise, the maximum period of provisional imprisonment shall be stipulated by law.

Article 18

1. The right to honor, to personal and family privacy and to the own image is guaranteed.

2. The home is inviolable. No entry or search may be made without the consent of the occupant or a legal warrant, except in cases of *flagrante delicto*.

3. Secrecy of communications is guaranteed, particularly of postal, telegraphic and telephonic communications, except in the event of a court order to the contrary.

4. The law shall limit the use of data processing in order to guarantee the honor and personal and family privacy of citizens and the full exercise of their rights.

Article 19

Spaniards have the right to choose their place of residence freely, and to move about freely within the national territory. Likewise, they have the right to freely enter and leave Spain subject to the conditions to be laid down by the law. This right may not be restricted for political or ideological reasons.

Article 20

1. The following rights are recognized and protected:

a) the right to freely express and disseminate thoughts, ideas and opinions trough words, in writing or by any other means of communication;

b) the right to literary, artistic, scientific and technical production and creation;

c) the right to academic freedom;

d) the right to freely communicate or receive accurate information by any means of dissemination whatsoever. The law shall regulate the right to invoke personal conscience and professional secrecy in the exercise of these freedoms.

2. The exercise of these rights may not be restricted by any form of prior censorship.

3. The law shall regulate the organization and parliamentary control of the social communications media under the control of the State or any public agency and shall guarantee access to such media to the main social and political groups, respecting the pluralism of society and of the various languages of Spain.

4. These freedoms are limited by respect for the rights recognized in this Title, by the legal provisions implementing it, and especially by the right to honor, to privacy, to personal reputation and to the protection of youth and childhood.

5. The confiscation of publications and recordings and other information media may only be carried out by means of a court order.

Article 21

1. The right to peaceful unarmed assembly is recognized. The exercise of this right shall not require prior authorization.

2. In the event of meetings in public places and of demonstrations, prior notification shall be given to the authorities, who may ban them only when there are well founded grounds to expect a breach of public order, involving danger to persons or property.

Article 22

1. The right of association is recognized.

2. Associations which pursue ends or use means classified as criminal offences are illegal.

3. Associations set up on the basis of this article must be recorded in a register for the sole purpose of public knowledge.

4. Associations may only be dissolved or have their activities suspended by virtue of a justified court order.

5. Secret and paramilitary associations are prohibited.

Article 23

1. Citizens have the right to participate in public affairs, directly or through representatives freely elected in periodic elections by universal suffrage.

2. They likewise have the right to access on equal terms to public office, in accordance with the requirements determined by law.

Article 24

1. Every person has the right to obtain the effective protection of the Judges and the Courts in the exercise of his or her legitimate rights and interests, and in no case may he go undefended.

2. Likewise, all persons have the right of access to the ordinary judge predetermined by law; to the defense and assistance of a lawyer; to be informed of the charges brought against them; to a public trial without undue delays and with full guarantees; to the use of evidence appropriate to their defense; to not make self-incriminating statements; to not declare themselves guilty; and to be presumed innocent. The law shall determine the cases in which, for reasons of family relationship or professional secrecy, it shall not be compulsory to make statements regarding alleged criminal offences.

Article 25

1. No one may be convicted or sentenced for any act or omission which at the time it was committed did not constitute a felony, misdemeanor or administrative offence according to the law in force at that time.

2. Punishments entailing imprisonment and security measures shall be aimed at rehabilitation and social reintegration and may not consist of forced labor. The person sentenced to prison shall enjoy during the imprisonment the fundamental rights contained in this Chapter except those expressly limited by the terms of the sentence, the purpose of the punishment and the penal law. In any case, he shall be entitled to paid employment and to the appropriate Social Security benefits, as well as to access to cultural opportunities and the overall development of his or her personality.

3. The Civil Administration may not impose penalties which directly or indirectly imply deprivation of freedom.

Article 26

Courts of Honor are prohibited within the framework of the Civil Administration and of professional associations.

Article 27

1. Everyone has the right to education. Freedom of teaching is recognized.

2. Education shall aim at the full development of the human character with due respect for the democratic principles of coexistence and for the basic rights and freedoms.

3. The public authorities guarantee the right of parents to ensure that their children receive religious and moral instruction that is in accordance with their own convictions.

4. Elementary education is compulsory and free.

5. The public authorities guarantee the right of everyone to education, through general education programming, with the effective participation of all parties concerned and the setting up of educational centers.

6. The right of individuals and legal entities to set up educational centers is recognized. provided they respect Constitutional principles.

7. Teachers, parents and, when appropriate, pupils, shall share in the control and management of all the centers maintained by the Administration out of public funds, under the terms established by the law.

8. The public authorities shall inspect and standardize the educational system in order to guarantee compliance with the law.

9. The public authorities shall give aid to teaching establishments which meet the requirements to be laid down by the law.

10. The autonomy of Universities is recognized, under the terms established by the law.

Article 28

1. Everyone has the right to freely join a trade union. The law may limit the exercise of this right or make an exception to it in the case of the Armed Forces or Institutes or other bodies subject to military discipline, and shall regulate the special conditions of its exercise by civil servants. Trade union freedom includes the right to set up trade unions

and to join the union of one's choice, as well as the right of the trade unions to form confederations and to found international trade union organizations, or to become members thereof. No one may be compelled to join a trade union.

2. The right of workers to strike in defense of their interests is recognized. The law regulating the exercise of this right shall establish the guarantees necessary to ensure the maintenance of essential community services.

Article 29

1. All Spaniards shall have the right to individual and collective petition, in writing, in the manner and subject to the consequences established by the law.

2. Members of the Armed Forces or Institutes or bodies subject to military discipline may only exercise this right individually and in accordance with the provisions of the legislation pertaining to them.

SECTION 2

Rights and duties of Citizens

Article 30

1. Citizens have the right and the duty to defend Spain.

2. The law shall determine the military obligations of Spaniards and shall regulate, with the proper safeguards, conscientious objection as well as other grounds for exemption from compulsory military service; it may also, when appropriate, impose a form of social service in lieu thereof.

3. A civilian service may be established with a view to accomplishing objectives of general interest.

4. The duties of citizens in the event of grave risk, catastrophe or public calamity may be regulated by law.

Article 31

1. Everyone shall contribute to sustain public expenditure in proportion to his or her financial means, through a just and progressive system of taxation based on principles of equality, which shall in no case be confiscatory in nature.

2. Public expenditure shall be incurred in such a way that an equitable allocation of public resources may be achieved, and its planning and execution shall comply with criteria of efficiency and economy.

3. Personal or property contributions for public purposes may only be imposed in accordance with the law

Article 32

1. Men and women have the right to marry with full legal equality.

2. The law shall regulate the forms of marriage, the age at which it may be entered into and the required capacity therefore, the rights and duties of the spouses, the grounds for separation and dissolution, and the consequences thereof.

Article 33

1. The right to private property and inheritance is recognized.

2. The content of these rights shall be determined by the social function which they fulfill, in accordance with the law.

3. No one may be deprived of his or her property and rights, except on justified grounds of public utility or social interest and with a proper compensation in accordance with the provisions of the law.

Article 34

1. The right to set up foundations for purposes of general interest is recognized, in accordance with the law.

2. The provisions of clauses 2 and 4 of Article 22 shall also be applicable to foundations.

Article 35

1. All Spaniards have the duty to work and the right to employment, to free choice of profession or trade, to advancement through their work, and to sufficient remuneration for the satisfaction of their needs and those of their families; moreover, under no circumstances may they be discriminated against on account of their gender.

2. The law shall establish a Workers' Statute.

Article 36

The law shall regulate the special features of the legal status of Professional Associations and the exercise of the professions requiring academic degrees. The internal structure and operation of the Associations must be democratic.

Article 37

1. The law shall guarantee the right to collective labor bargaining between worker and employer representatives, as well as the binding force of the agreements.

2. The right of workers and employers to adopt collective labor dispute measures is hereby recognized. The law regulating the exercise of this right shall, without prejudice to the restrictions which it may establish, include the safeguards necessary to ensure the operation of essential community services.

Article 38

Free enterprise is recognized within the framework of a market economy. The public authorities shall guarantee and protect its exercise and the safeguarding of productivity in accordance with the demands of the economy in general and, as the case may be, of its planning.

CHAPTER THREE

Governing Principles of Economic and Social Policy

Article 39

1. The public authorities shall ensure the social, economic and legal protection of the family.

2. The public authorities likewise shall ensure full protection of children, who are equal before the law, irrespective of their parentage and the marital status of the mothers. The law shall provide for the investigation of paternity.

3. Parents must provide their children, whether born within or outside wedlock, with assistance of every kind while they are still under age and in other circumstances in which the law is applicable.

4. Children shall enjoy the protection provided for in the international agreements which safeguard their rights.

Article 40

1. The public authorities shall promote favorable conditions for social and economic progress and for a more equitable distribution of personal and regional income within the framework of a policy of economic stability. They shall devote special attention to carrying out a policy directed towards full employment.

2. Likewise, the public authorities shall foster a policy guaranteeing vocational training and retraining; they shall ensure workplace safety and hygiene and shall guarantee adequate rest by means of a limited working day, periodic paid holidays, and the promotion of suitable centers.

Article 41

The public authorities shall maintain a public Social Security system for all citizens which will guarantee adequate social assistance and benefits in situations of hardship, especially in cases of unemployment. Supplementary assistance and benefits shall be optional.

Article 42

The State shall be especially concerned with safeguarding the economic and social rights of Spanish workers abroad, and shall direct its policy towards securing their return.

Article 43

1. The right to health protection is recognized.

2. It is incumbent upon the public authorities to organize and safeguard public health by means of preventive measures and the necessary benefits and services. The law shall establish the rights and duties of all concerned in this respect.

3. The public authorities shall promote health education, physical education and sports. Likewise, they shall encourage the proper use of leisure time.

Article 44

1. The public authorities shall promote and watch over access to cultural opportunities, to which all are entitled.

2. The public authorities shall promote science and scientific and technical research for the benefit the general interest.

Article 45

1. Everyone has the right to enjoy an environment suitable for personal development, as well as the duty to preserve it.

2. The public authorities shall safeguard rational use of all natural resources with a view to protecting and improving the quality of life and preserving and restoring the environment, by relying on essential collective solidarity.

3. Criminal or, where applicable, administrative sanctions, as well as the obligation to make good the damage, shall be imposed, under the terms established by the law, against those who violate the provisions contained in the previous clause.

Article 46

The public authorities shall guarantee the preservation and promote the enrichment of the historic, cultural and artistic heritage of the peoples of Spain and of the property of which it consists, regardless of its legal status and its ownership. Offences committed against this heritage shall be punished under criminal law.

Article 47

All Spaniards are entitled to enjoy decent and adequate housing. The public authorities shall promote the necessary conditions and shall establish appropriate standards in order to make this right effective, regulating land use in accordance with the general interest in order to prevent speculation.

The community shall participate in the benefits accruing from the urban policies of the public bodies.

Article 48

The public authorities shall promote conditions directed towards the free and effective participation of young people in political, social, economic and cultural development.

Article 49

The public authorities shall carry out a policy of preventive care, treatment, rehabilitation and integration of the physically, sensoriai and mentally handicapped who shall be given the specialized care that they require, and be afforded them special protection in order that they may enjoy the rights conferred by this Title upon all citizens.

Article 50

The public authorities shall guarantee, through adequate and periodically updated pensions, sufficient financial means for senior citizens. Likewise, and independently of the obligations of their families towards them, they shall promote their welfare through a system of social services which shall provide for their specific problems of health, housing, culture and leisure.

Article 51

1. The public authorities shall guarantee the protection of consumers and users and shall, by means of effective measures, safeguard their safety, health and legitimate financial interests.

2. The public authorities shall make means available to inform and educate consumers and users, shall foster their organizations, and shall provide hearings for such organizations on all matters affecting their members, under the terms to be established by law.

3. Within the framework of the provisions of the foregoing clauses, the law shall regulate domestic trade and the system of licensing commercial products.

Article 52

The law shall regulate professional organizations which contribute to the defense of their own economic interests. Their internal structure and operation must be democratic.

CHAPTER FOUR

Guarantee of Fundamental Rights and Liberties

Article 53

1. The rights and liberties recognized in Chapter Two of the present Title are binding for all public authorities. The exercise of such rights and liberties, which shall be protected in accordance with the provisions of Article 161, 1a), may be regulated only by law which shall, in any case, respect their essential content.

2. Any citizen may assert his or her claim to the protect the liberties and rights recognized in Article 14 and in Section 1 of Chapter Two, by means of a preferential and summary procedure in the ordinary courts and, when appropriate, by submitting an individual appeal for protection («recurso de amparo») to the Constitutional Court. This latter procedure shall be applicable to conscientious objection as recognized in Article 30.

3. The substantive legislation, judicial practice and actions of the public authorities shall be based on the recognition, respect and protection of the principles recognized in Chapter Three. The latter may only be invoked in the ordinary courts in the context of the legal provisions by which they are developed.

Article 54

An organic law shall regulate the institution of Ombudsman the People, who shall be a high commissioner of the Cortes Generales, appointed by them to defend the rights contained in this Title; for this purpose he may supervise Administration activities and report thereon to the Cortes Generales.

CHAPTER FIVE

Suspension of Rights and Liberties

Article 55

1. The rights recognized in Articles 17 and 18, clauses 2 and 3, Articles 19 and 20, clause 1, sub-clauses, a) and d) and clause 5, Articles 21 and 28, clause 2, and Article 37, clause 2, may be suspended when the state of emergency or siege (martial law) is declared under the terms provided in the Constitution. Clause 3 of Article 17 is excepted from the foregoing provisions in the event of the proclamation of a state of emergency.

2. An organic law may determine the manner and the circumstances in which, on an individual basis and with the necessary participation of the Courts and proper Parliamentary control, the rights recognized in Articles 17, clause 2, and 18, clauses 2 and 3, may be suspended as regards specific persons in connection with investigations of the activities of armed bands or terrorist groups. Unjustified or abusive use of the powers recognized in the foregoing organic law shall give rise to criminal liability where it is a violation of the rights and liberties recognized by the law.

APPENDIX

Selected Cases

Mr. Justice Clark delivered the opinion of the Court....

Today we once again examine *Wolfs* constitutional documentation of the right to privacy free from unreasonable state intrusion, and, after its dozen years on our books, are led by it to close the only courtroom door remaining open to evidence secured by official lawlessness in flagrant abuse of that basic right, reserved to all persons as a specific guarantee against that very same unlawful conduct. We hold that all evidence obtained by searches and seizures in violation of the Constitution is, by that same authority, inadmissible in a state court.

Since the Fourth Amendment's right of privacy has been declared enforceable against the States through the Due Process Clause of the Fourteenth, it is enforceable against them by the same sanction of exclusion as is used against the Federal Government...[T]he admission of the new constitutional right by *Wolf* could not consistently tolerate denial of its most important constitutional privilege, namely, the exclusion of the evidence which an accused had been forced to give by reason of the unlawful seizure. To hold otherwise is to grant the right but in reality to withhold its privilege and enjoyment...

Indeed, we are aware of no restraint, similar to that rejected today, conditioning the enforcement of any other basic constitutional right. The right to privacy, no less important than any other right carefully and particularly reserved to the people, would stand in marked contrast to all other rights declared as "basic to a free society." This Court has not hesitated to enforce as strictly against the State as it does against the Federal Government the rights of free speech and of a free press, the rights to notice and to a fair, public trial, including, as it does, the right not to be convicted by use of a coerced confession, however logically relevant it be, and without regard to its reliability....And nothing could be more certain than that when a coerced confession is involved, "the relevant rules of evidence" are overridden without regard to "the incidence of such conduct by the police," slight or frequent. Why should not the same rule apply to what is tantamount to coerced testimony by way of unconstitutional seizure of goods, papers, effects, documents, etc?...

The ignoble shortcut to conviction left open to the State tends to destroy the entire system of constitutional restraints on which the liberties of the people rest. Having once recognized that the right to privacy embodied in the Fourth Amendment is enforceable against the States and that the right to be secure against rude invasions of privacy by state officers is, therefore, constitutional in origin, we can no longer permit that right to be an empty promise. Because it is enforceable in the same manner and to like effect as other basic rights secured by the Due Process Clause, we can no longer permit it to be revocable as the whim of any police officer who, in the name of law enforcement itself, chooses to suspend its enjoyment. Our decision, founded on reason and truth, gives to the individual no more than that which the Constitution guarantees him, to the police officer no less than that to which honest law enforcement is entitled, and, to the courts, that judicial integrity so necessary in the true administration of justice....

Reversed and remanded.

Mr. Justice Black, concurring....[omitted].

Mr. Justice Douglas, concurring....[omitted].

Mr. Justice Stewart, concurring....[omitted].

Mr. Justice Harlan, whom Mr. Justice Frankfurter and Mr. Justice Whittaker join, dissenting....[omitted].

Griswold v. Connecticut
381 U.S. 479 (1965)

Mr. Justice Douglas delivered the opinion of the Court....

Coming to the merits, we are met with a wide range of questions that implicate the Due Process Clause of the Fourteenth Amendment. Overtones of some arguments suggest that *Lochner v. New York*.... should be our guide. But we decline that invitation....We do not sit as a super-legislature to determine the wisdom, need, and propriety of laws that touch economic problems, business affairs, or social conditions. This law, however, operates directly on an intimate relation of husband and wife and their physician's role in one aspect of that relation....

...[S]pecific guarantees in the Bill of Rights have penumbras, formed by emanations from those guarantees that help give them life and substance.... Various guarantees create zones of privacy. The right of association contained in the penumbra of the First Amendment is one.... The Third Amendment in its prohibition against the quartering of soldiers "in any house" in time of peace without the consent of the owner is another facet of that privacy. The Fourth Amendment explicitly affirms the "right of the people to be secure in their persons, houses, papers, and effects against unreasonable searches and seizures." The Fifth Amendment in its Self-Incrimination Clause enables the citizen to create a zone of privacy which government may not force him to surrender to his detriment. The Ninth Amendment provides: "The enumeration in the Constitution, of certain rights, shall not be construed to deny or disparage others retained by the people."....

The present case, then, concerns a relationship lying within the zone of privacy created by several fundamental constitutional guarantees. And it concerns a law which, in forbidding the *use* of contraceptives rather than regulating their manufacture or sale, seeks to achieve its goals by means having a maximum destructive impact upon that relationship. Such a law cannot stand in light of the familiar principle, so often applied by this Court, that a "governmental purpose to control or prevent activities constitutionally subject to state regulation may not be achieved by means which sweep unnecessarily broadly and thereby invade the area of protected freedom." Would we allow the police to search the sacred precincts of marital bedrooms for telltale signs of the use of contraceptives? The very idea is repulsive to the notions of privacy surrounding the marriage relationship.

We deal with a right of privacy older that the Bill of Rights – older than our political parties, older than our school system. Marriage is a coming together for better or for worse, hopefully enduring, and intimate to the degree of being sacred. It is an association that promotes a way of life, not causes; a harmony in living, not political faiths; a bilateral loyalty, not commercial or social projects. Yet it is an association for as noble a purpose as any involved in our prior decisions.

Reversed.

Mr. Justice Goldberg, whom the Chief Justice and Mr. Justice Brennan join, concurring....

The Ninth Amendment to the Constitution may be regarded by some as a recent discovery and may be forgotten by others, but since 1791 it has been a basic part of the Constitution which we are sworn to uphold. To hold that a right so basic and fundamental and so deep – rooted in our society as the right of privacy in marriage may be infringed because that right is not guaranteed in so many words by the first eight amendments to the Constitution is to ignore the Ninth Amendment and to give it no effect whatsoever....

Nor am I turning somersaults with history in arguing that the Ninth Amendment is relevant in a case dealing with a *State's* infringement of a fundamental right. While the Ninth Amendment – and indeed the entire Bill of Rights – originally concerned restrictions upon *federal* power, the subsequently enacted Fourteenth Amendment prohibits the States as well from abridging fundamental personal liberties. And, the Ninth Amendment, in indicating that not all such liberties are specifically mentioned in the first eight amendments, is surely relevant in showing the existence of other fundamental personal rights, now protected from state, as well as federal, infringement. In sum, the Ninth Amendment simply lends strong support to the view that "liberty" protected by the Fifth and Fourteenth Amendments from infringement by the Federal Government or the States is not restricted to rights specifically mentioned in the first eight amendments....

Mr. Justice Harlan, concurring in the judgement....

In my view, the proper constitutional inquiry in this case is whether this...statute infringes the Due Process Clause of the Fourteenth Amendment because the enactment violates basic values "implicit in the concept of ordered liberty." For reasons stated at length in my dissenting opinion in *Poe v Ullman*, I believe that it does. While the relevant inquiry may be aided by resort to one or more of the provisions of the Bill of Rights, it is not dependent on them or any of their radiations. The Due Process Clause... stands... on its own bottom....

While I could not more heartily agree that judicial "self restraint" is an indispensable ingredient of sound constitutional adjudication, ... the formula suggested for achieving it is more hollow than real. "Specific" provisions of of the Constitution, no less than "due process," lend themselves as readily to "personal" interpretations by judges whose constitutional outlook is simply to keep the Constitution in supposed "tune with the times."...

Judicial restraint will not... be brought about in the "due process" area by the historically unfounded incorporation formula long advanced by my Brother Black.... It will be achieved in this area... only by continual insistence upon respect for the teachings of history, solid recognition of the basic values that underlie our society, and wise appreciation of the great roles that the doctrines of federalism and separation of powers have played in establishing and preserving American freedoms. Adherence to these principles will not, of course, obviate all constitutional differences of opinion among judges, nor should it. Their continued recognition will, however, go farther toward keeping most judges from roaming at large in the constitutional field than will the interpolation into the Constitution of an artificial and largely illusory restriction on the content of the Due Process Clause.

Mr. Justice White, concurring...[omitted].

Mr. Justice Black, with whom Mr. Justice Stewart joins, dissenting.... **[omitted].**

Mr. Justice Stewart, with whom Mr. Justice Black joins, dissenting.... **[omitted].**

Miranda v Arizona
384 U.S. 436 (1966)

Mr. Chief Justice Warren delivered the opinion of the Court....

Our holding...briefly stated...is this: the prosecution may not use statements, whether exculpatory or inculpatory, stemming from custodial interrogation of the defendant unless it demonstrates the use of procedural safeguards effective to secure the privilege against self-incrimination. By custodial interrogation, we mean questioning initiated by law enforcement officers after a person has been taken into custody or otherwise deprived of his freedom of action in any significant way. As for the procedural safeguards to be employed, unless other fully effective means are devised to inform accused persons of their right of silence and to assure a continuous opportunity to exercise it, the following measures are required. Prior to any questioning, the person must be warned that he has a right to remain silent, that any statement he does make may be used as evidence against him, and that he has a right to the presence of an attorney, either retained or appointed. The defendant may waive effectuation of these rights, provided the waiver is made voluntarily, knowingly and intelligently. If, however, he indicates in any manner and at any stage of the process that he wishes to consult with an attorney before speaking there can be no questioning. Likewise, if the individual is alone and indicates in any manner that he does not wish to be interrogated, the police may not question him. The mere fact that he may have answered some questions or volunteered some statements on his own does not deprive him of the right to refrain from answering any further inquiries until he has consulted with an attorney and thereafter consents to be questioned.

The constitutional issue we decide in each of these cases is the admissibility of statements obtained from a defendant questioned while in custody and deprived of his freedom of action. In each, the defendant was questioned by police officers, detectives, or a prosecuting attorney in a room in which he was cut off from the outside world. In none of these cases was the defendant given a full and effective warning of his rights at the outset of the interrogation process. In all the cases, the questioning elicited oral admissions, and in three of them, signed statements as well which were admitted at their trials. They all thus share salient features – incommunicado interrogation of individuals in a police – dominated atmosphere, resulting in self – incriminating statements without full warnings of constitutional rights.

An understanding of the nature and setting of this in – custody interrogation is essential to our decisions today....

...[T]he modern practice of in – custody interrogation is psychologically rather than physically oriented.... Interrogation still takes place in privacy. Privacy results in secrecy and this in turn results a gap in our knowledge as to what in fact goes on in the interrogation rooms. A valuable source of information about present police practices, however, may be found in various police manuals and texts which document procedures employed with success in the past, and which recommend various other effective tactics....

From these representative samples of interrogation techniques, the setting prescribed by the manuals and observed in practice becomes clear. In essence, it is this: To be alone with the subject is essential to prevent distraction and to deprive him of any outside support. The aura of confidence in his guilt undermines his will to resist. He merely confirms the preconceived story the police seek to have him describe. Patience and persistence, at times relentless questioning, are employed. To obtain a confession, the interrogator must "patiently maneuver himself or his quarry into a position from which the desired object may be obtained." When normal procedures fail to produce the needed result, the police may resort to deceptive stratagems such as giving false legal advice. It is important to keep the subject off balance, for example, by trading on his insecurity about himself or his surroundings. The police then persuade, trick, or cajole him out of exercising his constitutional rights.

Even without employing brutality, the "third degree" or the specific stratagems described above, the very fact of custodial interrogation exacts a heavy toll on individual liberty and trades on the weakness of individuals.

In these cases, we might not find the defendants' statements to have been involuntary in traditional terms. Our concern for adequate safeguards to protect precious Fifth Amendment rights is, of course, not lessened in the slightest. To be sure, the records do not evince overt physical coercion or patented psychological ploys. The fact remains that in none of these cases did the officers undertake to afford appropriate safeguards at the outset of the interrogation to insure that the statements were truly the product of free choice....

Today... there can be no doubt that the Fifth Amendment privilege is available outside of criminal court proceedings and serves to protect persons in all settings in which their freedom of action is curtailed from being compelled to incriminate themselves....

The circumstances surrounding in – custody interrogation can operate very quickly to overbear the will of one merely made aware of his privilege by his interrogators. Therefore, the right to have counsel present at the interrogation is indispensable to the protection of Fifth Amendment privilege under the system we delineate today. Our aim is to assure that the individual's right to choose between silence and speech remains unfettered throughout the interrogation process....

Our decision is not intended to hamper the traditional function of police officers in investigating crime.... General on – the – scene questioning as to facts surrounding a crime or other general questioning of citizens in the fact – finding process is not affected by our holding. It is an act of responsible citizenship for individuals to give whatever information they may have to aid in law enforcement. In such situations the compelling atmosphere inherent in the process of in – custody interrogation is not necessarily present.

In dealing with statements obtained through interrogation, we do not purport to find all confessions inadmissible. Confessions remain a proper element in law enforcement. Any statement given freely and voluntarily without any compelling influences is, of course, admissible in evidence. The fundamental import of the privilege while an individual is in custody is not whether he is allowed to talk to the police without the benefit of warnings and counsel, but whether he can be interrogated. There is no requirement that police stop a person who enters a police station and states that he wishes to confess to a crime, or a person who calls the police to offer a confession or any other statement he desires to make. Volunteered statements of any kind are not barred by the Fifth Amendment and their admissibility is not affected by our holding today....

It is so ordered.

Mr. Justice Clark, dissenting... [omitted]
Mr. Justice Harlan, whom Mr. Justice Stewart and Mr. Justice White join, dissenting... [omitted]

Brown v. Board of Education
347 U.S. 483 (1954)

Mr. Chief Justice Warren delivered the opinion of the Court.

These cases come to us from the states of Kansas, South Carolina, Virginia, and Delaware. They are premised on different facts and different local conditions, but a common legal question justifies their consideration together in this consolidated opinion.

In each of the cases, minors of the Negro race, through their legal representatives, seek the aid of the courts in obtaining admission to the public schools of their community on a nonsegregated basis. In each instance, they had been denied admission to schools attended by white children under laws requiring or permitting segregation according to race.

This segregation was alleged to deprive the plaintiffs of the equal protection of the laws under the Fourteenth Amendment. In each of the cases other than the Delaware case, a three-judge Federal District Court denied relief to the plaintiffs on the so-called "separate but equal" doctrine, announced by this court in *Plessy v. Ferguson....*

The plaintiffs contend that segregated public schools are not "equal" and cannot be made "equal," and that, hence, they are deprived of the equal protection of the laws. Because of the obvious importance of the question presented, the Court took jurisdiction. Argument was heard in the 1952 term, and reargument was heard this term on certain questions propounded by the Court.

Reargument was largely devoted to the circumstances surrounding the adoption of the Fourteenth Amendment in 1868. It covered, exhaustively, consideration of the Amendment in Congress, ratification by the states, then existing practices in racial segregation, and the views of proponents and opponents of the Amendment.

This discussion and our own investigation convinced us that, although these sources cast some light, it is not enough to resolve the problem with which we are faced.

At best, they are inconclusive. The most avid proponents of the postwar Amendments undoubtedly intended them to remove all legal distinctions among "all persons born or naturalized in the United States."

Their opponents, just as certainly, were antagonistic to both the letter and the spirit of the Amendments and wished them to have the most limited effect. What others in Congress and the State legislatures had in mind cannot be determined with any degree of certainty.

An additional reason for the elusive nature of the Amendment's history, with respect to segregated schools, is the status of public education at that time. In the South, the movement toward free common schools, supported by general taxation, had not yet taken hold. Education of white children was largely in the hands of private groups. Education of Negroes was almost nonexistent, and practically all of the race was illiterate. In fact, any education of Negroes was forbidden by law in some states....

As a consequence, it is not surprising that there should so little in the history of the Fourteenth Amendment relating to its intended effect on public education....

In approaching this problem, we cannot turn the clock back to 1868 when the Amendment was adopted, or even to 1896, when *Plessy v. Ferguson* was written. We must consider public education in the light of its full development and its present place in American life throughout the nation. Only in this way can it be determined if segregation in public schools deprives these plaintiffs of the equal protection of the laws.

Today, education is perhaps the most important function of state and local governments. Compulsory school attendance laws and the great expenditures for education both demonstrate our recognition of the importance of education to our democratic society. It is required in the performance of our most basic public responsibilities, even service in the armed forces. It is the very foundation of good citizenship.

Today, it is a principal instrument in awakening the child to cultural values, in preparing him for later professional training, and in helping him to adjust normally to his environment.

In these days, it is doubtful that any child may reasonably be expected to succeed in life if he is denied the opportunity of an education. Such an opportunity, where the state has undertaken to provide it, is a right which must be made available to all on equal terms.

We come then to the question presented: Does segregation in public schools solely on the basis of race, even though the physical facilities and other "tangible" factors may be equal, deprive the children of the minority group of equal educational opportunities? We believe that it does.

In *Sweatt v. Painter*.... in finding that a segregated law school for Negroes could not provide them equal educational opportunities, this court relied on large part on "those qualities which are incapable of objective measurement but which make for greatness in a law school."

In *McLaurin v. Oklahoma State Regents*... the court, in requiring that a Negro admitted to a white graduate school be treated like all other students, again resorted to intangible considerations: "...his ability to study, engage in discussions and exchange views with other students, and, in general, to learn his profession."

Such considerations apply with added force to children in grade and high schools. To separate them from others of similar age and qualifications solely because of their race generates a feeling of inferiority as to their status in the community that may affect their hearts and minds in a way unlikely ever to be undone....

Whatever may have been the extent of psychological knowledge at the time of *Plessy v. Ferguson*, this finding is amply supported by modern authority.

...Any language in *Plessy v. Ferguson* contrary to this finding is rejected.

We conclude that in the field of public education the doctrine of "separate but equal" has no place. Separate educational facilities are inherently unequal. Therefore, we hold that the plaintiffs and others similarly situated for whom the actions have been brought are, by reason of the segregation complained of, deprived of the equal protection of the laws guaranteed by the Fourteenth Amendment...

We have now announced that such segregation is a denial of the equal protection of the laws. In order that we may have the full assistance of the parties in formulating decrees the cases will be restored to the docket, and the parties are requested to present further argument Questions 4 and 5 previously propounded by the court for the reargument this Term.....

It is so ordered.

Regina v. Oakes
(1986) 26 D.L.R. (4th) 200

Supreme Court of Canada, Dickson C.J.C., Estey, McIntyre, Chouinard, Lamer, Wilson and Le Dain JJ. February 28, 1986......

Dickson C.J.C.: - This appeal concerns the constitutionality of s.8 of the *Narcotic Control Act*, R.S.C. 1970, c. N-1. The section provides, in brief, that if the court finds the accused in possession of a narcotic, he is presumed to be in possession for the purpose of trafficking. Unless the accused can establish the contrary, he must be convicted of trafficking. The Ontario Court of Appeal held that this provision constitutes a "reverse onus" clause and is unconstitutional because it violates one of the core values of our criminal justice system, the presumption of innocence, now entrenched in s.11 (d) of the *Canadian Charter of Rights and Freedoms*. The Crown has appealed.....

The presumption of innocence is a hallowed principle lying at the very heart of criminal law. Although protected expressly in s.11 (d) of the Charter, the presumption of innocence is referable and integral to the general protection of life, liberty and security of the person contained in s.7 of the Charter......The presumption of innocence protects the fundamental liberty and human dignity of any and every person accused by the State of criminal conduct. An individual charged with a criminal offence faces grave social and personal consequences, including potential loss of physical liberty, subjection to social stigma and ostracism from the community, as well as other social, psychological and economic harms. In light of the gravity of these consequences, the presumption of innocence is crucial. It ensures that until the State proves an accused's guilt beyond all reasonable doubt, he or she is innocent. This is essential in a society committed to fairness and social justice. The presumption of innocence confirms our faith in humankind; if reflects our belief that individuals are decent and law-abiding members of the community until proven otherwise.....

In light of the above, the right to be presumed innocent until proven guilt requires that s.11 (d) have, at a minimum, the following content. First, an individual must be proven guilty beyond a reasonable doubt. Secondly, it is the State which must bear the burden of proof.......Thirdly; criminal prosecutions must be carried out in accordance with lawful procedures and fairness. The latter part of s.11 (d), which requires the proof of guilt "according to law in a fair and public hearing by an independent and impartial tribunal", underlines the importance of this procedural requirement.....

Although there are important lessons to be learned from the *Canadian Bill of Rights* jurisprudence, it does not constitute binding authority in relation to the constitutional interpretation of the Charter.....

.....In Canada, we have tempered parliamentary supremacy by entrenching important rights and freedoms in the Constitution. Viscount Sankey's statutory exception proviso is clearly not applicable in this context and would subvert the very purpose of the entrenchment of the presumption of innocence in the Charter. I do not, therefore, feel constrained in this case by the interpretation of s.2 (f) of the *Canadian Bill of Rights* presented in the majority judgement in *Appleby*. Section 8 of the *Narcotic Control Act* is not rendered constitutionally valid simply by virtue of the fact that it is a statutory provision.....

In the United States, protection of the presumption of innocence is not explicit. Rather, it has been read into the "due process" provisions contained in the Fifth and Fourteenth Amendments of the American Bill of Rights....

To return to s.8 of the *Narcotic Control Act*, I am in no doubt whatsoever that it violates s.11 (d) of the Charter by requiring the accused to prove on a balance of probabilities that he was not in possession of the narcotic for the purpose of trafficking. Mr. Oakes is compelled by s.8 to prove he is *not* guilty of the offence of trafficking. He thus denied his right to be presumed innocent and subjected to the potential penalty of life imprisonment unless he can rebut the presumption. This is radically and fundamentally inconsistent with the societal values of human dignity and liberty which we espouse, and is directly contrary to the presumption of innocence enshrined in s.11 (d). Let us turn now to s.1 of the Charter.

V

Is s.8 of the Narcotic Control Act a reasonable and demonstrably justified limit pursuant to s.1 of the Charter?

The Crown submits that even if s.8 of the *Narcotic Control Act* violates s.11 (d) of the Charter, it can still be upheld as a reasonable limit under s.1 which, as has been mentioned, provides:

The *Canadian Charter of Rights and Freedoms* guarantees the rights and freedoms set out in it subject only to such reasonable limits prescribed by law as can be demonstrably justified in a free and democratic society. The question whether the limit is "prescribed by law" is not contentious in the present case since s.8 of the *Narcotic Control Act* is a duly enacted legislative provision. It is, however, necessary to determine if the limit on Mr. Oakes' right, as guaranteed by s.11 (d) of the Charter, is "reasonable" and "demonstrably justified in a free and democratic society" for the purpose of s.1 of the Charter, and thereby saved from inconsistency with the Constitution.

It is important to observe at the outset that s.1 has two functions: first, it constitutionally guarantees the rights and freedoms set out in the provisions which follow; and, secondly, it states explicitly the exclusive justificatory criteria (outside of s.33 of the Charter) against which limitations on those rights and freedoms must be measured. Accordingly, any s.1 inquiry must be premised on an understanding that the impugned limit violates constitutional rights and freedoms – rights and freedoms which are part of the supreme law of Canada.....

Having outlined the general principles of s.1 inquiry, we must apply them to s.8 of the *Narcotic Control Act*. Is the reverse onus provision in s.8 a reasonable limit on the right to be presumed innocent until proven guilty beyond a reasonable doubt as can be demonstrably justified in a free and democratic society?

The starting point for formulating a response to this question is, as stated above, the nature of Parliament's interest or objective which accounts for the passage of s.8 of the *Narcotic Control Act*. According to the Crown, s.8 of the *Narcotic Control Act* is aimed at curbing drug trafficking by facilitating the conviction of drug traffickers. In my opinion Parliament's concern that drug trafficking be decreased can be characterized as substantial and pressing.....

The next stage of inquiry is a consideration of the means chosen by Parliament to achieve its objective. The means must be reasonable and demonstrably justified in a free and democratic society. As outlined above, this proportionality test should begin with a consideration of rationality of the provision: is the reverse onus clause in s.8 rationally related to the objective of curbing drug trafficking? At a minimum, this requires that s.8 be internally rational; there must be a rational connection between the basic fact of possession and the presumed fact of possession for the purpose of trafficking. Otherwise, the reverse onus clause could give rise to unjustified and erroneous convictions for drug trafficking of persons guilty only of possession of narcotics.

In my view, s.8 does not survive this rational connection test.....

VI

Conclusion

The Ontario Court of Appeal was correct in holding that s.8 of the *Narcotic Control Act* violates the *Canadian Charter of Rights and Freedoms* and is therefore of no force or effect. Section 8 imposes a limit on the right guaranteed by s.11 (d) of the Charter which is not reasonable and is not demonstrably justified in a free and democratic society for the purpose of s.1. Accordingly, the constitutional question is answered as follows:

Question: Is s.8 of the *Narcotic Control Act* inconsistent with s.11 (d) of the *Canadian Charter of Rights and Freedoms* and thus of no force and effect?

Answer: Yes

I would, therefore, dismiss the appeal.

ESTEY J.: I would dismiss this appeal......
McINTYRE J. concurs with ESTEY J.
CHOUINARD, LAMER, WILSON, and LE DAIN JJ. Concur with DICKSON C.J.C.

Appeal dismissed.

JUDGMENT – 1:   **COOKE P:....**

The Canadian Charter of Rights and Freedoms *enacted by the* Constitution Act
1982, *contains a provision, s. 10 (b), closely corresponding to s. 23 (1) (b) of the*
New Zealand Bill of Rights Act. The provisions are not identical, but for present
purposes there is no material difference. The Canadian Criminal Code provides
for tests by roadside screening devices and breathalysers. Broadly they
correspond to the New Zealand Transport Act provisions for breath-screening
tests and evidential breath tests.

In R v. Therens *[1985] 18 DLR (4th) 655; 45 CR (3d) 97 the Supreme Court of*
Canada held that requirement made of a motorist that he accompany a police
officer to a police station to submit to a breathalyser test had the result that he
was "detained" and that in that case the defendant's Charter right to be informed
of his rights to retain and instruct counsel without delay had been violated....

In R v. Thomsen *[1988] 63 CR (3d) 1 the Supreme Court was concerned with*
roadside screening devices. A different result was reached. It was held that a
demand to accompany a police officer to a police car resulted in detention, but
that the scheme of the legislation showed that the roadside test was to be
administered as quickly as possible...

There are three relevant differences between the Canadian Charter *and the* New
Zealand Bill of Rights Act. *First, the Canadian Charter is supreme law,*
overriding inconsistent legislation, whereas in New Zealand legislation is not
invalid if inconsistent with the Bill of Rights Act (s. 4). Secondly, the New Zealand
Act enacts in s. 6 the following rule of interpretation, a ruling having no
counterpart in the Canadian Charter:

"6. Interpretation consistent with Bill of Rights to be preferred – Wherever an
enactment can be given a meaning that is consistent with the rights and freedoms
contained in this Bill of Rights, that meaning shall be preferred to any other
meaning."

Thirdly, the New Zealand Act contains no express provision about remedies or the exclusion of evidence.....

Notwithstanding the various differences between the Canadian Charter *and the* New Zealand Bill of Rights Act *the argument for the appellants in these cases was that as regards the testing of drivers for alcohol the same result should be reached in New Zealand as in Canada. In the light of the scheme and operating requirements of the Transport Act, it was not contended that there is any right to legal advice at the stage of a breath-screening test. But it was contended that the scheme and operating requirements are not inconsistent with a right to legal advice at the evidential breath test stage. If so, before submitting to an evidential breath test, the person is entitled to be informed of his right to consult and instruct a lawyer without delay, and to be given a reasonable opportunity of exercising that right. It was accepted that a reasonable opportunity to consult by telephone would be enough. That acceptance is in accord with a long line of Canadian authority, under both the Charter and the former Bill of Rights 1960, that a reasonable opportunity of telephone consultation is or may be enough, although there is no "one call" rule....*

On the other hand the main argument for the Crown is that, as to evidential breath tests and blood tests as well as breath-screening tests, the scheme and operating requirements of the Transport Act impliedly exclude s. 23 (1) (b) of the Bill of Rights Act and the right to legal advice altogether.....

Part II of the New Zealand Bill of Rights Act *sets out the rights and freedoms affirmed by the Act. The drafting is of the kind typical of declarations of human rights, described by Lord Wilberforce giving the judgement of the Privy Council in Minister of Home Affairs v. Fisher (1980).... as "a broad and ample style which lays down principles of width and generality". Section 23 (1) (b) has been quoted at the outset of this judgment. There is no need to quote any of the other provisions of Part II. In the Fisher case, which concerned the Bermuda Constitution, Lord Wilberforce after referring to the European Convention for Protection of Human Rights and Fundamental Freedoms (1953) and the United Nations' Universal Declaration of Human Rights (1948) made the statement, now evidently destined for judicial immortality:*

"These antecedents, and the form of Chapter 1 itself, call for a generous interpretation avoiding what has been called 'the austerity of tabulated legalism,'

suitable to give to individuals the full measure of the fundamental rights and freedoms referred to."

In Flickinger v. Crown Colony of Hong Kong *(1991) ... this Court held that the same approach should be applied s. 23 of the New Zealand Act....*

...Counsel for the Crown urged us not to take the open mind approach in interpreting the New Zealand Bill of Rights Act, *on the ground that it is not a constitutional document. They also cautioned that the New Zealand Courts should not adopt what they called "the rhetoric" of some Canadian Supreme Court judgments.*

The warning against rhetoric I will strive to observe, without overlooking that we in New Zealand may be able to learn from the Supreme Court of Canada. They have had much more experience than the New Zealand Courts in dealing with declarations of rights. A debate about the two possible approaches seems of minimal importance in the context of the present case. Perhaps there will be some cases where the difference becomes significant, but it would seem implausible to suggest that the meaning in a declaration of rights of words such as "arrested" .... or "detained" or "consult and instruct" should vary according whether or not the declaration is part of an entrenched constitution...

As Barker J pointed out in Re S [1992] ....the long title shows that, in affirming the rights and freedoms contained in the Bill if Rights, the Act requires development of the law where necessary. Such a measure is not to be approached as if it did no more than preserve the status quo.... Internationally there is now general recognition that some human rights are fundamental and anterior to any municipal law, although municipal law may fall short of giving effect to them: .... The right to legal advice on arrest or detention under an enactment may not be quite in that class, but in any event it has become a widely–recognised right... and one of those affirmed in New Zealand. It has great "strategic" value as a safeguard against violations of undoubtedly fundamental rights such as the right not to be arbitrarily arrested or detained (s. 22 of the New Zealand Bill of Rights Act). Subject to contrary requirements in any legislation, the New Zealand Courts must now, in my opinion, give it practical effect irrespective of the state of our law before the Bill of Rights Act.

What is practical effect can only be a question of fact dependent on the particular circumstances. As in innumerable situations with which the law has to deal, a test of reasonableness naturally fails to be applied. A person arrested or detained is not entitled to abuse his or her right. Anyone who deliberately delays will forfeit Bill of Rights Act protection. In the present cases it is conceded for the appellants that before evidential breath tests or blood tests under the Transport Act a reasonable opportunity of consultation with a lawyer by telephone is enough. Telephone consultation would not always be enough for a person held on a charge of murder, for instance. The effect of the Bill of Rights Act will have to be worked out with common sense....

...The rights and freedoms in Part II are not constitutionally entrenched and may be overridden by an ordinary enactment, but in interpreting an enactment a consistent meaning is to be preferred to any other meaning. The preference will come into play only when the enactment can be given a meaning consistent with the rights and freedoms....

...Most countries with which New Zealand had affinity, probably all, have both laws of some kind protecting human rights and laws against drunken driving. The two have to be reconciled. Under the New Zealand system, which does not give rights the primacy given by some other systems, in the end the question is fairly simple. It reduces to whether the right to a reasonable opportunity of obtaining legal advice by telephone is inconsistent with the scheme of the Transport Act regarding evidential breath tests and blood tests.

...There is no solid ground for inferring that the administration of the Transport Act will be substantially impaired or the road toll substantially reduced by the time required to give drivers who have been duly brought in for further tests, usually after a positive breath screening test, a limited opportunity of making telephone contact with a lawyer and taking advice. In relation to evidential breath tests and blood tests the two Acts can reasonably stand together....

Consequently I would hold that Curran's refusal of a blood test and Noort's furnishing of an evidential breath test each followed a violation of the Bill of Rights Act. At least unless it can safely be assumed that the failure to comply with the Bill of Rights Act did not contribute to cause the subsequent refusal or test, both the latter should prima facie be ruled out as evidence. Absence of causation cannot safely be assumed: legal advice, even of an elementary kind, might have helped the persons detained to decide whether to elect to undergo the tests or to face the consequences of prosecutions for refusing....

....[I] have no doubt that it is consistent with the Bill of Rights Act to say at least that evidence obtained immediately after a violation should not be admitted unless the prosecution proves that it would have been forthcoming or discovered whether or not there had been a violation. The burden is not discharged in either of these cases....

[Judgments of Richardson, Hardie Boys, McKay JJ concurring and Gault J dissenting – Omitted]

Disposition: **Appeals allowed; convictions quashed.**

Simpson v Attorney-General [Baigent's Case]
Court of Appeal, Wellington
[1994] 3 NZLR 667

JUDGEMENT - 1:   **COOKE P: ....**

...The appeal raises important issues concerning police powers, including whether monetary compensation can be awarded for infringement of the rights affirmed by the New Zealand Bill of Rights Act 1990, *s. 21:*

21. Unreasonable search and seizure - - Everyone has the right to be secure against unreasonable search or seizure, whether of the person, property, or correspondence or otherwise.

Accordingly each of the five members of the Court who sat in the case is delivering a separate judgement. In the event, however, there is a wide measure of agreement....

First cause of action: negligent application for search warrant.

The plaintiffs allege that before applying for the search warrant the Detective Constable failed to exercise reasonable care to ascertain O'Brien's correct address..... This alleged cause of action was rightly struck out.

Second cause of action: trespass on land and in house.

The plaintiffs plead in the amended statement of claim of 27 March 1992 that in entering on or remaining on or searching the property at 16 London Road Korokoro the police officers acted without lawful justification, not bona fide, and maliciously.....

....On this appeal we are concerned with the pleadings only. It seems to me that on the facts pleaded there is ground for the view that, after having entered the property, the police realised or ought to have realised that the warrant contained or probably contained the wrong address: and that, if acting in good faith and fairly and reasonably, they ought at least to have desisted until the situation was clarified. An application for the summary remedy of striking out should not be governed by fine distinctions. Consequently, in so far as the second cause of action depends on tortious conduct by the police party, I think it is tenable.

But there is a deeper difficulty. Individual police officers are not parties to the proceeding. It is the Attorney-General who is sued. By the *Crown Proceedings Act 1950*, s. 6 (10 (a), subject to the provisions of that Act and any other Act, the Crown is subject to all those liabilities in tort to which, if it were a private person of full age and capacity, it would be subject in respect of torts committed by its servants or agents....

The Crown argues, and the argument was accepted by the High Court Judge and the Master, that the search warrant was judicial process and that therefore the Crown is not vicariously liable under s. 6.

In common with all my colleagues and Greig J and Master Williams, I accept that the warrant was judicial process, being issued out of a Court and being granted by a person required to consider the application judicially and in substance acting for that purpose as a judicial officer....

In this situation I think that the solution is dictated by s. 6 of the *New Zealand Bill of Rights Act 1990*, which, where an enactment can be given a meaning that is consistent with the rights and freedoms contained in the Bill of Rights, requires that meaning to be preferred to any other meaning. I accept that this legislative injunction does not extend to a strained meaning: but the principle that a generally-worded protection does not cover acts done in bad faith has respectable support: to apply it is not to strain. Taken together, ss. 3 and 21 of the Bill of Rights Act affirm security against unreasonable search or seizure on behalf of the executive branch of the Government of New Zealand (which must include the police). It is consistent with that affirmed right to interpret s. 6 (5) of the *Crown Proceedings Act* as not protecting the Crown from liability for the execution of a search warrant in bad faith.

But it would be strained, in my opinion, to go further and hold that s. 6 (5) does not cover an unreasonable execution of a search warrant carried out in good faith. That seems to be an example of the very kind of vicarious liability which the subsection is intended to exclude. So I think that the second cause of action would not be maintainable in so far as unreasonableness simpliciter is alleged (as in the proposed first amended statement of claim).....

The pleaded allegation that in the circumstances the officers did not have lawful justification may be allowed to stand, as there is a tenable argument that, if the officers realized that O'Brien did not live at 16 London Road, the warrant no longer gave them lawful authority to search that address. If so, whether s. 6 (5) of the *Crown Proceedings Act* would exclude vicarious liability is a question best left, I think, until precise findings of fact are made. In the meantime I prefer to express no opinion on it.

Third cause of action: misfeasance in public office.

The plaintiffs plead that the police officers abused the process of execution of a search warrant and were guilty of misfeasance in public office.... The third cause of action, as pleaded, can therefore be left standing, but in my opinion it will not succeed without proof of bad faith or (assuming that there is a difference) realization by the officers that O'Brien did not live at the address and continuance of the search thereafter.

Fourth cause of action in proposed first amended statement of claim: trespass to goods of second plaintiff.

Similar considerations appear to me to apply. The cause of action proposed to be introduced will be sustainable only if bad faith is proved or possibly if it is held that the warrant ceased to be available because, before interfering with the son's possessions, the officers realized that it was not O'Brien's address.

Last cause of action: breach of New Zealand Bill of Rights.

This claim raises the most important issue in the appeal. The plaintiffs plead that in entering on or remaining on or searching the property in the circumstances described the officers conducted an unreasonable search in violation of s. 21 of the *New Zealand Bill of Rights Act*.

In previous Bill of Rights cases I have tried to emphasize the importance of a straightforward and generous approach to the provisions of the Act. There is no need to labour that theme further. I repeat only two observations which I ventured to make in *Ministry of Transport v. Noort* [1992] ..., and from which no member of the Court appears to have differed. First, although the New Zealand Act contains no express provision about remedies, this is probably not of much consequence. Subject to ss. 4 and 5, the rights and freedoms in Part II have been affirmed as part of the fabric of New Zealand law. The ordinary range of remedies will be available for their enforcement and protection. Secondly, the long title shows that, in affirming the rights and freedoms contained in the Bill of Rights, the Act requires development of the law when necessary. Such a measure is not to be approached as if it did no more than preserve the status quo.

Hitherto the main remedy granted for breaches of the rights and freedoms has been the exclusion of evidence. But that has been because most of the cases have concerned evidence obtained unlawfully; exclusion has been the most effective redress and ample to do justice. In other jurisdictions compensation is a standard remedy for human rights violations. There is no reason for New Zealand jurisprudence to lag behind. The possibility of compensation for breach of the Bill of Rights, in a sufficiently meritorious case, was alluded to in Noort at p. 275, and there were also some cautious observations on the subject in *Sharma v. ANZ Banking Group* (New Zealand) Ltd. [1990-92] ..., a case of uncertain merit.

It is argued for the Crown that the absence of a remedies clause in the Bill of Rights Act is significant, particularly by contrast with the inclusion of one in the draft Bill in the White Paper "A Bill of Rights for New Zealand" of 1985, which was not proceeded with. As indicated in Noort, I do not attach weight to this argument. By its long title the Act is "(a) To affirm, protect, and promote human rights and fundamental freedoms in New Zealand". The words "protect" and "promote" are as strong as the word "vindicate" which, as the case law cited in the judgment to be delivered by Hardie Boys J shows, has influenced the Irish Courts in granting a compensation remedy despite the absence of a remedies clause. The New Zealand Act is " (b) To affirm New Zealand's commitment to the International Covenant on Civil and Political Rights". By art. 2(3) of the Covenant each state party has undertaken inter alia to ensure an effective remedy for violation (those are equally strong words) and to develop the possibilities of judicial remedy. Article 17 includes the right not to be subjected to arbitrary or unlawful interference with privacy and home.

Section 3 of the New Zealand Act make it clear that the Act binds the Crown in respect of functions of the executive government and its agencies. It "otherwise specially provides" within the meaning of s. 5 (k) of the Acts Interpretation Act 1924. Section 3 also makes it clear that the Bill of Rights applies to acts done by the Courts. The Act is binding on us, and we would fail in our duty if we did not give an effective remedy to a person whose legislatively affirmed rights have been infringed. In a case such as the present the only effective remedy is compensation. A mere declaration would be toothless. In other cases a mandatory remedy such as an injunction or an order for return of property might be appropriate: compare *Magana v. Zaire* [1983] 2 Selected Decisions of the Human Rights Committee (under the Optional Protocol)…

It is necessary to be alert in New Zealand to the danger that both the Courts and Parliament at times may give, or at least be asked to give, lip service to human rights in high-sounding language, but little or no real service in terms of actual decisions. If so, it is a natural tendency or temptation for those adjusting to Bill of Rights concepts, perhaps excusable on that account but still to be guarded against…..

Section 21 of the Bill of Rights Act assures protection against unreasonable search or seizure. The enactments already mentioned, namely s. 6 (5) of the Crown Proceedings Act 1950, and the sections in the Crimes Act 1961 and the Police Act 1958, contain exemptions from certain liabilities; but none of them is directed to Bill of Rights liability. More over, the effect of s. 6 of the Bill of Rights Act is that they are all to be given, so far as reasonably possible, a meaning consistent with the rights affirmed in s. 21. Section 5 of the Bill of Rights Act allows for reasonable limits prescribed by law (which of course includes judicial decision) on the rights and freedoms contained in the Bill of Rights, if the limits can be demonstrably justified in a free and democratic society.….

As to the level of compensation, on which again there is much international case law, I think that it would be premature at this stage to say more than that, in addition to any physical damage, intangible harm such as distress and injured feelings may be compensated for; the gravity of the breach and the need to emphasize the importance of the affirmed rights and to deter breaches are also proper considerations; but extravagant awards are to be avoided. If damages are awarded on causes of action not based on the Bill of Rights, they must be allowed for in any award of compensation under the Bill of Rights so that there will be no double recovery. A legitimate alternative approach, having the advantage of simplicity, would be to make a global award under the Bill of Rights and nominal or concurrent awards on any other successful causes of action…..

In accordance with the opinion of the majority of the Court, the appeal is allowed by reinstating against the first defendant the amended statement of claim of 27 March 1992 except as to the first cause of action pleaded. The latter will remain struck out…

[Judgments by Casey, Hardie Boys, Gault, and Mckay JJ concurring – Omitted]

Disposition: ***Appeal allowed in part***

Justice O'Connor delivered the opinion of the Court....

We last addressed the use of race in public higher education over 25 years ago. In the landmark *Bakke* case, we reviewed a racial set-aside program that reserved 16 out of 100 seats in a medical school class for members of certain minority groups. The decision produced six separate opinions, none of which commanded a majority of the Court. Four Justices would have upheld the program against all attack on the ground that the government can use race to "remedy disadvantages cast on minorities by past prejudice." Four other Justices avoided the constitutional question altogether and struck down the program on [Title VI] statutory grounds. Justice Powell provided a fifth vote not only for invalidating the set-aside program, but also for reversing the state court's injunction against any use of race whatsoever. The only holding for the Court in *Bakke* was that a "state has a substantial interest that legitimately may be served by a properly devised admissions program involving the competitive consideration of race and ethnic origin." Thus, we reversed that part of the lower court's judgment that enjoined the university "from any consideration of the race of any applicant."

Since this Court's splintered decision in *Bakke*, Justice Powell's opinion announcing the judgment of the Court has served as the touchstone for constitutional analysis of race-conscious admissions policies…We therefore discuss Justice Powll's opinion in some detail.

In Justice Powell's view, when governmental decisions "touch upon an individual's race or ethnic background, he is entitled to a judicial determination that the burden he is asked to bear on that basis is precisely tailored to serve a compelling governmental interest." Under this exacting standard, only one of the interests asserted by the university survived Justice Powell's scrutiny.

First, Justice Powell rejected an interest in "reducing the historic deficit of traditionally disfavored minorities in medical schools and in the medical profession" as an unlawful interest in racial balancing. Second, Justice Powell rejected an interest in remedying societal discrimination because such measures would risk placing unnecessary burdens on innocent third parties "who bear no responsibility for whatever harm the beneficiaries of the special admissions program are thought to have suffered." Third, Justice Powell rejected an interest in "increasing the number of physicians who will practice in communities currently underserved," concluding that even if such an interest could be compelling in some circumstances, the program under review was not "geared to promote that goal."

Justice Powell approved the university's use of race to further only one interest: "the attainment of a diverse student body."

Justice Powell was, however, careful to emphasize that in his view race "is only one element in a range of factors a university properly may consider in attaining the goal of a heterogeneous student body."...

[F]or the reasons set out below, today we endorse Justice Powell's view that student body diversity is a compelling state interest that can justify the use of race in university admissions.

The Equal Protection Clause provides that no State shall "deny to any person within its jurisdiction the equal protection of the laws." Because the Fourteenth Amendment "protect[s] persons, not groups," all "governmental action based on race – a group classification long recognized as in most circumstances irrelevant and therefore prohibited – should be subjected to detailed judicial inquiry to ensure that the personal right to equal protection of the laws has not been infringed." ...It follows from that principle that "government may treat people differently because of their race only for the most compelling reasons."

We have held that all racial classifications imposed by government "must be analyzed by a reviewing court under strict scrutiny." This means that such classifications are constitutional only if they are narrowly tailored to further compelling governmental interests....

Although all governmental uses of race are subject to strict scrutiny, not all are invalidated by it...Context matters when reviewing race-based governmental action under the Equal Protection Clause...Not every decision influenced by race is equally objectionable, and strict scrutiny is designed to provide a framework for carefully examining the importance and the sincerity of the reasons advanced by the governmental decision-maker for the use of race in that particular context.

With these principles in mind, we turn to the question whether the Law School's use of race is justified by a compelling state interest.

[T]he Law School asks us to recognize, in the context of higher education, a compelling state interest in student body diversity...Today, we hold that the Law School has a compelling interest in attaining a diverse student body.

The Law School's educational judgment that such diversity is essential to its educational mission is one to which we defer...Our scrutiny of the interest asserted by the Law School is no less strict for taking into account complex educational judgments in an area that lies primarily within the expertise of the university...

As part of its goal of "assembling a class that is both exceptionally academically qualified and broadly diverse," the Law School seeks to "enroll a 'critical mass' of minority students." The Law School's interest is not simply "to assure within it student body some specified percentage of a particular group merely because of its race or ethnic origin."...Rather, the Law School's concept of critical mass is defined by reference to the educational benefits that diversity is designed to produce.

These benefits are substantial...[T]he Law School's admissions policy promotes "cross-racial understanding," helps to break down racial stereotypes, and "enables [students] to better understand persons of different races."... [N]umerous studies show that student body diversity promotes learning outcomes, and "better prepares students for an increasingly diverse workforce and society, and better prepares them as professionals."...

These benefits are not theoretical but real, as major American businesses have made clear that the skills needed in today's increasingly global marketplace can only be developed through exposure to widely diverse people, cultures, ideas, and viewpoints. What is more, high-ranking retired officers and civilian leaders of the United States military assert that, "[b]ased on [their] decades of experience," a "highly qualified, racially diverse officer corps...is essential to the military's ability to fulfill its principle mission to provide national security."...

Even in the limited circumstance when drawing racial distinctions is permissible to further a compelling state interest, government is still "constrained in how it may pursue that end: [T]he means chosen to accomplish the [government's] asserted purpose must be specifically and narrowly framed to accomplish that purpose."...

We find that the Law School's admissions program bears the hallmarks of a narrowly tailored plan. As Justice Powell made clear in Bakke, truly individualized consideration demands that race be used in a flexible, non-mechanical way. It follows from this mandate that universities cannot establish quotas for members of certain racial groups or put members of those groups on separate admissions tracks. Nor can universities insulate applicants who belong to certain racial or ethnic groups from the competition for admission. Universities can, however, consider race or ethnicity more flexibly as a "plus" factor in the context of individualized consideration of each and every applicant...

The Law School's goal of attaining a critical mass of underrepresented minority students does not transform its program into a quota...

163

Here, the Law School engages in a highly individualized, holistic review of each applicant's file, giving serious consideration to all the ways an applicant might contribute to a diverse educational environment. The Law School affords this individualized consideration to applicants of all races. There is no policy, either *dejure* or *defacto*, of automatic acceptance or rejection based on any single "soft" variable...All applicants have the opportunity to highlight their own potential diversity contributions through the submission of a personal statement, letters of recommendation, and an essay describing the ways in which the applicant will contribute to the life and diversity of the Law School.

Petitioner and the United States argue that the Law School's plan is not narrowly tailored because race-neutral means exist to obtain the educational benefits of student body diversity that the Law School seeks. We disagree. Narrow tailoring does not require exhaustion of every conceivable race-neutral alternative. Nor does it require a university to choose between maintaining a reputation for excellence or fulfilling a commitment to provide educational opportunities to members of all racial groups...

We agree with the Court of Appeals that the Law School sufficiently considered workable race-neutral alternatives. The District Court took the Law School to task for failing to consider race-neutral alternatives such as "using a lottery system" or "decreasing the emphasis for all applicants on undergraduate GPA and LSAT scores." But these alternatives would require a dramatic sacrifice of diversity, the academic quality of all admitted students, or both.

We acknowledge that "there are serious problems of justice connected with the idea of preference itself." Narrow tailoring, therefore, requires that a race-conscious admissions program not unduly harm members of any racial group...To be narrowly tailored, a race-conscious admissions program must not "unduly burden individuals who are not members of the favored racial and ethnic groups." We are satisfied that the Law School's admissions program does not...

We are mindful, however, that "[a] core purpose of the Fourteenth Amendment was to do away with all governmentally imposed discrimination based on race."...We see no reason to exempt race-conscious admissions programs from the requirement that all governmental use of race must have a logical end point....

In the context of higher education, the durational requirement can be met by sunset provisions in race-conscious admissions policies and periodic reviews to determine whether racial preferences are still necessary to achieve student body diversity...

It has been 25 years since Justice Powell first approved the use of race to further an interest in student body diversity in the context of public higher education. Since that time, the number of minority applicants with high grades and test scores has indeed increased. We expect that 25 years from now, the use of racial preferences will no longer be necessary to further the interest approved today.

In summary, the Equal Protection Clause does not prohibit the Law School's narrowly tailored use of race in admissions decisions to further a compelling interest in obtaining the educational benefits that flow from a diverse student body. Consequently, petitioner's statutory claims based on Title VI also fail...The judgment of the Court of Appeals for the Sixth Circuit, accordingly, is affirmed.

....It is so ordered.

The dissenting opinion of Chief Justice Rehnquist, with whom Justice Scalia, Justice Kennedy, and Justice Thomas join....
...omitted...

Justice Kennedy delivered the opinion of the Court....

These cases require us to consider the validity of the Partial-Birth Abortion Ban Act of 2003...We conclude the Act should be sustained against the objections lodged by the broad, facial attack brought against it...

Between 85 and 90 percent of the approximately 1.3 million abortions performed each year in the United States take place in the first three months of pregnancy...The most common first-trimester abortion method is vacuum aspiration (otherwise known as suction curettage) in which the physician vacuums out the embryonic tissue...

Of the remaining abortions that take place each year, most occur in the second trimester. The surgical procedure referred to as "dilation and evacuation" or "D&E" is the usual abortion method in this trimester...

The abortion procedure that was impetus for the numerous bans on "partial-birth abortion," including the Act, is a variation of this standard D&E. The medical community has not reached unanimity on the appropriate name for this D&E variation. It has been referred to as "intact D&E," "dilation and extraction" (D&X), and "intact D&X." [T]his D&E variation will be referred to as intact D&E. The main difference between the two procedures is that in intact D&E a doctor extracts the fetus intact or largely intact with only a few passes. There are no comprehensive statistics indicating what percentage of all D&Es are performed in this manner...

In an intact D&E procedure the doctor extracts the fetus in a way conducive to pulling out its entire body, instead of ripping it apart...

Whatever one's views concerning the *Casey* (1992) joint opinion, it is evident a premise central to its conclusion – that the government has a legitimate and substantial interest in preserving and promoting fetal life – would be repudiated were the Court now to affirm the judgments of the Courts of Appeals...

We assume the following principles for the purposes of this opinion. Before viability, a State "may not prohibit any woman from making the ultimate decision to terminate her pregnancy." It also may not impose upon this right an undue burden, which exists if a regulation's "purpose or effect is to place a substantial obstacle in the path of a woman seeking an abortion before the fetus attains viability." On the other hand, "[r]egulations which do no more than create a structural mechanism by which the State, or the parent or guardian of a minor, may express profound respect for the life of the unborn are permitted, if they are not a substantial obstacle to the woman's exercise of the right to choose. Casey, in short, struck a balance. The balance was central to its holding. We now apply its standard to the cases at bar...

[T]he Act's text demonstrates its purpose and the scope of its provisions: It regulates and proscribes, with exceptions or qualifications to be discussed, performing the intact D&E procedure...In this litigation the Attorney General does not dispute that the Act would impose an undue burden if it covered standard D&E.

We conclude that the Act is not void for vagueness, does not impose an undue burden from any overbreadth, and is not invalid on its face...

First, the person performing the abortion must "vaginally delive[r] a living fetus."...

Second, the Act's definition of partial-birth abortion requires the fetus to be delivered "until, in the case of a head-first presentation, the entire fetal head is outside the body of the mother, or, in the case of breech presentation, any part of the fetal trunk past the naval is outside the body of the mother."...

Third, to fall within the Act, a doctor must perform an "overt act, other than completion of delivery, that kills the partially delivered living fetus." For purposes of criminal liability, the overt act causing the fetus' death must be separate from delivery. And the overt act must occur after the delivery to an anatomical landmark...

Fourth, the Act contains scienter requirements concerning all the actions involved in the prohibited abortion...If a living fetus is delivered past the critical point by accident or inadvertence, the Act is inapplicable. In addition, the fetus must have been delivered "for the purpose of performing an overt act that the [doctor] knows will kill [it]." If either intent is absent, no crime has occurred...

The Act provides doctors "of ordinary intelligence a reasonable opportunity to know what is prohibited."...Unlike the statutory language in Stenberg that prohibited the delivery of a "substantial portion" of the fetus – where a doctor might question how much of the fetus is a substantial portion – the Act defines the line between potentially criminal conduct on the one hand and lawful abortion on the other. Doctors performing D&E will know that if they do not deliver a living fetus to an announced landmark, they will not face criminal liability...

We next determine whether the Act imposes an undue burden, as a facial matter, because its restrictions on second-trimester abortions are too broad. A review of the statutory text discloses the limits of its reach. The Act prohibits intact D&E; and, notwithstanding respondents' arguments, it does not prohibit the D&E procedure in which the fetus is removed in parts...

The Act makes the distinction the Nebraska statute failed to draw (but the Nebraska Attorney General advanced) by differentiating between the overall partial-birth abortion and the distinct overt act that kills the fetus. The fatal overt act must occur after delivery to an anatomical landmark, and it must be something" other than [the] completion of delivery." This distinction matters because, unlike intact D&E, standard D&E does not involve a delivery followed by a fatal act...

The abortions affected by the Act's regulations take place both previability and postviability; so the ...question is whether the Act, measured by its text in this facial attack, imposes a substantial obstacle to late-term, but previability, abortions. The Act does not on its face impose a substantial obstacle, and we reject this further facial challenge to its validity.

The Act proscribes a method of abortion in which a fetus is killed just inches before completion of the birth process. The Act expresses respect for the dignity of human life...

The government may use its voice and its regulatory authority to show its profound respect for the life within the woman...Where it has a rational basis to act, and it does not impose an undue burden, the State may use its regulatory power to bar certain procedures and substitute others, all in furtherance of its legitimate interests in regulating the medical profession in order to promote respect for life, including life of the unborn.

The Act's ban on abortions that involve partial delivery of a living fetus furthers the Government's objectives. No one would dispute that, for many, D&E is a procedure itself laden with the power to devalue human life...

Respect for human life finds an ultimate expression in the bond of love the mother has for her child. The Act recognizes this reality as well. Whether to have an abortion requires a difficult and painful moral decision. While we find no reliable data to measure the phenomenon, it seems unexceptionable to conclude some women come to regret their choice to abort the infant life they once created and sustained...

It is objected that the standard D&E is in some respects as brutal, if not more, than the intact D&E, so that the legislation accomplishes little. What we have already said, however, shows ample justification for the regulation. Partial-birth abortion, as defined by the Act, differs from a standard D&E because the former occurs when the fetus is partially outside the mother to the point of one of the Act's anatomical landmarks. It was reasonable for Congress to think that partial-birth abortion, more than standard D&E, "undermines the public's perception of the appropriate role of a physician during the delivery process, and perverts a process during which life is brought into the world." There would be a flaw in this Court's logic, and an irony in its jurisprudence, were we first to conclude a ban on both D&E and intact D&E was overbroad and then to say it is irrational to ban only intact D&E because that does not prescribe both procedures...

The Act's furtherance of legitimate government interests bears upon, but does not resolve, the next question: whether the Act has the effect of imposing an unconstitutional burden on the abortion right because it does not allow use of the barred procedure where "necessary, in appropriate medical judgment, for [the] preservation of the ...health of the mother." The prohibition in the Act would be unconstitutional, under precedents we here assume to be controlling, if it "subject[ed] [women] to significant health risks."...

There is documented medical disagreement whether the Act's prohibition would ever impose significant health risks on women...

The question becomes whether the Act can stand when this medical uncertainty persists...The Court has given state and federal legislatures wide discretion to pass legislation in areas where there is medical and scientific uncertainty... "When Congress undertakes to act in areas fraught with medical and scientific uncertainties, legislative options must be especially broad."... Physicians are not entitled to ignore regulations that direct them to use reasonable alternative procedures. The law need not give abortion doctors unfettered choice in the course of their medical practice, nor should it elevate their status above other physicians in the medical community...

Alternatives are available to the prohibited procedure...If the intact D&E procedure is truly necessary in some circumstances, it appears likely an injection that kills the fetus is an alternative under the Act that allows the doctor to perform the procedure...

The considerations we have discussed support our further determination that these facial attacks should not have been entertained in the first instance. In these circumstances the proper means to consider exceptions is by as-applied challenge. The Government has acknowledged that pre-enforcement, as-applied challenges to the Act can be maintained. This is the proper manner to protect the health of the woman if it can be shown that in discrete and well-defined instances a particular condition has or is likely to occur in which the procedure prohibited by the Act must be used. In an as-applied challenge the nature of the medical risk can be better quantified and balanced than in a facial attack...

[R]espondents have not demonstrated that the Act would be unconstitutional in a large fraction of relevant cases. We note that the statute here applies to all instances in which the doctor proposes to use the prohibited procedure, not merely those in which the woman suffers from medical complications. It is neither our obligation nor within our traditional institutional role to resolve questions of constitutionality with respect to each potential situation that might develop...

Respondents have not demonstrated that the Act, as a facial matter, is void for vagueness, or that it imposes an undue burden on a woman's right to abortion based on its overbreadth or lack of a health exception. For these reasons the judgments of the Courts of Appeals for the Eighth and Ninth Circuits are reversed.

It is so ordered.

The concurring opinion of Justice Thomas, with whom Justice Scalia joins.
...omitted

The dissenting opinion of Justice Ginsburg, with whom Justices Stevens, Souter, and Breyer join.
...omitted

Justice Stevens announced the judgment of the Court and delivered the opinion of the Court with respect to most of the excerpted passages below.

Petitioner Salim Ahmed Hamdan, a Yemeni national, is in custody at an American prison in Guantanamo Bay, Cuba. In November 2001, during hostilities between the United States and the Taliban (which then governed Afghanistan), Hamdan was captured by militia forces and turned over to the U.S. military. In June 2002, he was transported to Guantanamo Bay. Over a year later, the President deemed him eligible for trial by military commission for then-unspecified crimes. After another year had passed, Hamdan was charged with one count of conspiracy "to commit...offenses triable by military commission."

Hamdan ...concedes that a court-martial constituted in accordance with the Uniform Code of Military Justice (UCMJ) would have authority to try him. His objection is that the military commission the President has convened lacks such authority, for two principal reasons: First, neither congressional Act nor the common law of war supports trial by this commission for the crime of conspiracy – an offense that, Hamdan says, is not a violation of the law of war. Second, Hamdan contends, the procedures that the President has adopted to try him violate the most basic tenets of military and international law, including the principle that a defendant must be permitted to see and hear the evidence against him.

The District Court granted Hamdan's request for a writ of habeas corpus (2004). The Court of Appeals for the District of Columbia Circuit reversed (2005)....[W]e granted certiorari.

For the reasons that follow, we conclude that the military commission convened to try Hamdan lacks power to proceed because its structure and procedures violate both the UCMJ and the Geneva Conventions. Four of us also conclude that the offense with which Hamdan has been charged is not an "offens[e] that by...the law of war may be tried by military commissions."

[T]he Government filed a motion to dismiss the writ of certiorari. The ground cited for dismissal was the recently enacted Detainee Treatment Act of 2005 (DTA). We postponed our ruling on that motion pending argument on the merits, and now deny it.

The DTA, which was signed into law on December 30, 2005, addresses a broad swath of subjects related to detainees...Section 2241 of title 28, United States Code, is amended by adding at the end the following: "Except as provided in section 1005 of the Detainee Treatment Act of 2005, no court, justice, or judge shall have jurisdiction to hear or consider – an application for a writ of habeas corpus filed by or on behalf of an alien detained by the Department of Defense at Guantanamo Bay, Cuba…This section shall take effect on the date of the enactment of this Act…"

The Government argues that [the DTA] had the immediate effect, upon enactment, of repealing federal jurisdiction not just over detainee habeas actions yet to be filed but also over such actions then pending in any federal court – including this Court. Accordingly, it argues, we lack jurisdiction to review the Court of Appeals' decision below.

Hamdan objects to this theory on both constitutional and statutory grounds. Principal among his constitutional arguments is that the Government's preferred reading raises grave questions about Congress' authority to impinge upon this Court's appellate jurisdiction, particularly in habeas cases…Hamdan also suggests that, if the Government's reading is correct, Congress has unconstitutionally suspended the writ of habeas corpus.

We find it unnecessary to reach either of these arguments. Ordinary principles of statutory construction suffice to rebut the Government's theory – at least insofar as this case, which was pending at the time the DTA was enacted is concerned…

For these reasons, we deny the Government's motion to dismiss.

The Constitution makes the President the "Commander in Chief" of the Armed Forces, but vests in Congress the powers to "declare War…and make Rules concerning Captures on Land and Water," to "raise and support Armies," to "define and punish…Offenses against the Law of Nations," and "to make Rules for the Government and Regulation of the land and naval Forces." The interplay between these powers was described by Chief Justice Chase in the seminal case of *Ex parte Milligan*…

Whether Chief Justice Chase was correct in suggesting that the President may constitutionally convene military commissions "without the sanction of Congress" in cases of "controlling necessity" is a question this Court has not answered definitively, and need not answer today. For we held in [Ex parte] *Quirin* that Congress had, through Article of War 15, sanctioned the use of military commissions in such circumstances… Article 21 of the UCMJ, the language of which is substantially identical to the old Article 15 was preserved by Congress after World War II.….

We have no occasion to revisit *Quirin's* controversial characterization of Article of War 15 as congressional authorization for military commissions. Contrary to the Government's assertion, however, even *Quirin* did not view the authorization as a sweeping mandate for the President to "invoke military

172

commissions when he deems them necessary." Rather, the *Quirin* Court recognized that Congress had simply preserved what power, under the Constitution and the common law of war, the President had had before 1916 to convene military commissions – with the express condition that the President and those under his command comply with the law of war. That much is evidenced by the Court's inquiry, following its conclusion that Congress had authorized military commissions, into whether the law of war had indeed been complied with in that case.

The Government would have us dispense with the inquiry that the *Quirin* Court undertook and find in either the AUMF or the DTA specific, overriding authorization for the very commission that has been convened to try Hamdan. Neither of these congressional Acts, however, expands the President's authority to convene military commissions...Absent a more specific congressional authorization, the task of this Court is, as it was in *Quirin*, to decide whether Hamdan's military commission is so justified. It is to that inquiry we now turn...

Quirin is the model the Government invokes most frequently to defend the commission convened to try Hamdan...[N]o more robust model of executive power exists...

At a minimum, the Government must make a substantial showing that the crime for which it seeks to try a defendant by military commission is acknowledged to be an offense against the law of war. That burden is far from satisfied here...

In sum...the Government has failed even to offer a "merely colorable" case for inclusion of conspiracy among those offenses cognizable by law-of-war military commission. Because the charge does not support the commission's jurisdiction, the commission lacks authority to try Hamdan...

Whether or not the Government has charged Hamdan with an offense against the law of war cognizable by military commission, the commission lacks power to proceed. The UCMJ conditions the President's use of military commissions on compliance not only with the American common law of war, but also with the rest of the UCMJ itself, insofar as applicable, and with the "rules and precepts of the law of nations," – including, *inter alia*, the four Geneva Conventions signed in 1949. The procedures that the Government has decreed will govern Hamdan's trial by commission violate these laws.

The commission's procedures are set forth in Commission Order No. 1, which was amended most recently on August 31, 2005 – after Hamdan's trial had already begun... The accused also is entitled to a copy of the charge(s) against him...and to certain other rights typically afforded criminal defendants in civilian courts and courts-martial. These rights are subject, however, to one glaring condition: The accused and his civilian counsel may be excluded from, and precluded from ever learning what evidence was presented during, any part of the proceeding that either the Appointing Authority or the presiding officer decides to "close."... Appointed military defense counsel must be privy to these closed sessions, but may, at the presiding officer's discretion, be forbidden to reveal to his or her client what took place therein.

Another striking feature of the rules governing Hamdan's commission is that they permit the admission of any evidence that, in the opinion of the presiding officer, "would have probative value to a reasonable person." Under this test, not only is testimonial hearsay and evidence obtained through coercion fully admissible, but neither live testimony nor witnesses' written statements need be sworn. Moreover, the accused and his civilian counsel may be denied access to evidence in the form of "protected information"...so long as the presiding officer concludes that the evidence is "probative" and that its admission without the accused's knowledge would not "result in the denial of a full and fair trial."...

In part because the difference between military commissions and the courts-martial originally was a difference of jurisdiction alone, and in part to protect against abuse and ensure evenhandedness under the pressures of war, the procedures governing trials by military commission historically have been the same as those governing courts-martial...

The uniformity principle is not an inflexible one; it does not preclude all departures from the procedures dictated for use by courts-martial. But any departure must be tailored to the exigency that necessitates it. That understanding is reflected in Article 36 of the UCMJ...

Article 36 places two restrictions on the President's power to promulgate rules of procedure for courts-martial and military commissions alike. First, no procedural rule he adopts may be "contrary to or inconsistent with" the UCMJ – however practical it may seem. Second, the rules adopted must be "uniform insofar as practicable." That is, the rules applied to military commissions must be the same as those applied to courts-martial unless such uniformity proves impracticable.

Hamdan argues that Commission Order No. 1 violates both of these restrictions; he maintains that the procedures described in the Commission Order are inconsistent with the UCMJ and that the Government has offered no explanation for their deviation from the procedures governing courts-martial, which are set forth in the Manual for Courts-Martial...Without reaching the question whether any provision of Commission Order No. 1 is strictly "contrary to or inconsistent with" other provisions of the UCMJ, we conclude that the "practicability" determination the President has made is insufficient to justify variances from the procedures governing courts-martial...Nothing in the record before us demonstrates that it would be impracticable to apply court-martial rules in this case...

Under the circumstances, then, the rules applicable in courts-martial must apply. Since it is undisputed that Commission Order No. 1 deviates in many significant respects from those rules, it necessarily violates Article 36(b)...

The conflict with al Qaeda is not, according to the Government, a conflict to which the full protections afforded detainees under the 1949 Geneva Conventions apply because Article 2 of those Conventions (which appears in all four Conventions) renders the full protections applicable only to "all cases of declared war or of any other armed conflict which may arise between two or more of the High Contracting Parties." Since Hamdan was captured and detained incident to the conflict with al Qaeda and not the conflict with the Taliban, and since al Qaeda, unlike Afghanistan, is not a "High Contracting party" – that is, a signatory of the Conventions, the protections of those Conventions are not, it is argued, applicable to Hamdan.

We need not decide the merits of this argument because there is at least one provision of the Geneva Conventions that applies here even if the relevant conflict is not one between signatories. Article3, often referred to as Common Article 3 because, like Article 2, it appears in all four Geneva Conventions, provides that in a "conflict not of an international character occurring in the territory of one of the High Contracting Parties, each Party to the conflict shall be bound to apply, as a "minimum," certain provisions protecting "[p]ersons taking no active part in the hostilities, including members of armed forces who have laid down their arms and those placed *hors de combat* by...detention." One such provision prohibits "the passing of sentences and the carrying out of executions without previous judgment pronounced by a regularly constituted court affording all the judicial guarantees which are recognized as indispensable by civilized peoples."...

Common Article 3, then, is applicable here and...requires that Hamdan be tried by a "regularly constituted court affording all the judicial guarantees which are recognized as indispensable by civilized peoples." While the term "regularly constituted court" is not specifically defined in either Common Article 3 or its accompanying commentary, other sources disclose its core meaning...At a minimum, a military commission "can be 'regularly constituted' by the standards of our military justice system only if some practical need explains deviations from court-martial practice."...

Inextricably intertwined with the question of regular constitution is the evaluation of the procedures governing the tribunal and whether they afford "all the judicial guarantees which are recognized as indispensable by civilized peoples." Like the phrase "regularly constituted court," this phrase is not defined in the text of the Geneva Conventions. But it must be understood to incorporate at least the barest of those trial protections that have been recognized by customary international law...[The] procedures adopted to try Hamdan deviate from those governing courts-martial in ways not justified by any "evident practical need," and for that reason, at least, fail to afford the requisite guarantees...[A]t least absent express statutory provision to the contrary, information used to convict a person of a crime must be disclosed to him.

Common Article 3 obviously tolerates a great degree of flexibility in trying individuals captured during armed conflict; its requirements are general ones, crafted to accommodate a wide variety of legal systems. But *requirements* they are nonetheless. The commission that the President has convened to try Hamdan does not meet those requirements....[I]n undertaking to try Hamdan and subject him to criminal punishment, the Executive is bound to comply with the Rule of Law that prevails in this jurisdiction.

The judgment of the Court of Appeals is reversed, and the case is remanded for further proceedings.

It is so ordered.

Concurring opinion of Justice Kennedy, with whom Justices Souter, Ginsburg, and Breyer join in art, concurring in part...
    ....omitted

Dissenting opinion of Justice Thomas, with whom Justice Scalia joins, and with whom Justice Alito joins in part...
    ....omitted